THE POCKET
UNIVERSAL
METHODS
OF DESIGN

100 Ways to Research Complex Problems, Develop
Innovative Ideas, and Design Effective Solutions

Bella Martin   Bruce Hanington

ROCKPORT

Contents

A/B Testing

Comparing two versions of a design to see which performs better against a predetermined goal

- A/B testing is an optimization technique that allows you to compare two different versions of a design to see which one gets you closer to a business objective.

- Tests are run by randomly assigning different people down two paths—the "A" test and the "B" test—until a statistically relevant sample size is reached.

- Testing can assess design aspects such as different treatments of text copy (tone, length, and font size); form elements (how many, layout, and which are required); and different treatments of the button or call to action (page placement, size, color, and labeling).

- A/B testing won't help you understand why the design was preferred over the alternate, so pair it with qualitative methods to gain a deeper understanding of customer trust, desires, attitudes, and needs.

See also　Experiments • Key Performance Indicators • Web Analytics

An eBay study comparing image size determined that users were more engaged with larger images, even though it sacrificed the amount of information contained to one page, contradicting research expectations.

AEIOU

A framework for structuring field observations

- This can be used to guide any ethnographic or observational method, corresponding to five interrelated elements:

  - **Activities** are goal-directed sets of actions or the pathways that people take toward the things they want to accomplish.

  - **Environments** include the context in which activities take place, including the atmosphere and function of individual and shared spaces.

  - **Interactions** are the routine and special exchanges between people and between people and objects in the environment.

  - **Objects** are the key elements of the environment, sometimes put to complex or even unintended uses.

  - **Users** are the people whose behaviors, preferences, and needs are being observed, including their roles and relationships.

See also   Contextual Inquiry • Fly-on-the-Wall Observation • Observation

Fieldwork observations of Activities, Environments, Interactions, Objects, and Users are converged onto a team worksheet for synthesis and analysis by the design team.

Affinity Diagramming

The visible clustering of observations and insights into meaningful categories and relationships

- Designers capture research insights, observations, concerns, or requirements on individual sticky notes.

- Rather than grouping notes into predefined categories, specific details are clustered, which then give rise to named category themes based on shared affinity of similar intent, issues, or problems.

- Making tacit knowledge or information buried in transcripts visible facilitates research synthesis.

- Affinity diagramming from contextual inquiry is based on interviews and observations of users in the field, synthesizing human stories.

- Affinity diagramming from usability testing documents observations and quotes of participant task performance to determine priority issues to be fixed.

- Color-coded sticky notes can help to efficiently parse information by user, task, or issue.

See also   Contextual Design • KJ Technique • Content Analysis

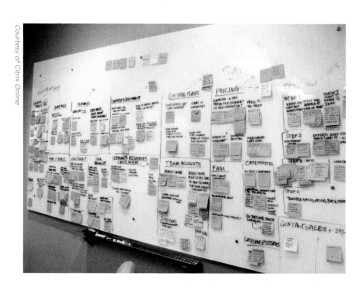

Observations from multiple usability tests at Citrix are color-coded by participant, prioritizing issues to be revised and retested.

Artifact Analysis

A systematic examination of the material, aesthetic, and interactive qualities of objects

- It asks what objects say about people and their culture, time, and place rather than focusing on what people say about the products and systems they use.

- Material analysis addresses the quantity, material composition, physical and digital components, durability, wear patterns, and disposability of objects.

- Aesthetic analysis includes subjective assessment of form, color, texture, references to particular eras, time, or place, and emotional significance.

- Interactive aspects of the analysis address the characteristics of operational use and behaviors that the artifact affords: for example, function and complexity.

- Contextual aspects include where objects are stored or carried, if they are part of a larger whole, and if they are owned, shared, public, or private property.

- Identifying object misuse or adapted use can suggest design opportunities.

See also Personal Inventories • Touchstone Tours • Unobtrusive Measures

Artifact analysis is a systematic examination of the material, aesthetic, and interactive qualities of objects in context.

Automated Remote Research

Using web-based tools to reveal statistically relevant data for usability enhancements

- Enables design teams to leverage web-based tools to collect statistically significant information about what people are doing on your website or web application.

- Focus is on planning the appropriate strategy for the study, accurately selecting the right automated remote research tools, and configuring the logistics.

- Automated research tools can help researchers understand usability issues such as length of time and performance on task, common click paths, and trouble spots.

- It should be used with qualitative research methods that provide insight into why site visitors behave the way they do.

- Quantitative data can be triangulated with observed behavioral data to decide which usability enhancements to make.

- There a growing number of web-based research tools available that are both quantitative and qualitative.

See also   Crowdsourcing • Experiments • Remote Moderated Research

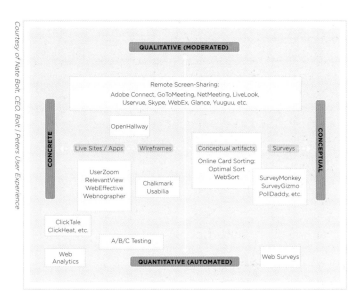

QUALITATIVE (MODERATED)

CONCRETE

CONCEPTUAL

Remote Screen-Sharing:

Adobe Connect, GoToMeeting, NetMeeting, LiveLook, Uservue, Skype, WebEx, Glance, Yuuguu, etc.

OpenHallway

Live Sites / Apps   Wireframes   Conceptual artifacts   Surveys

UserZoom
RelevantView
WebEffective
Webnographer

Chalkmark
Usabilia

Online Card Sorting:
Optimal Sort
WebSort

SurveyMonkey
SurveyGizmo
PollDaddy, etc.

ClickTale
ClickHeat, etc.

A/B/C Testing

Web
Analytics

QUANTITATIVE (AUTOMATED)

Web Surveys

This is a framework of different types of remote research tools and applications. Automated remote methods are shown towards the bottom half of the diagram.

Behavioral Mapping

Systematic visual documentation of location-based human activity

- This is used to document observable human activities and personal characteristics, interactions, time spent at fixed locations or in transit, and details of environmental context.

- A sketch map or architectural floor plan is used as the underlay for recording observations.

- Place-centered mapping is based on observations of all people and their interactions at a specific location.

- Individual-centered mapping follows the travel and activities of specific individuals over time and location, documenting their social behaviors and interactions.

- While typically completed in real time, mapping can involve time-lapse photography or video.

- Interviews or debriefing conversations with participants help to understand more about mapped behaviors.

- In retrospective mapping, individuals chart their own paths and behaviors on a floor plan or map, revealing their motivations for actions.

See also Fly-on-the-Wall Observation • Shadowing • Unobtrusive Measures

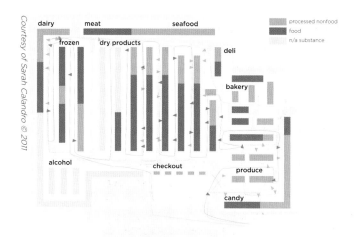

dairy   meat   seafood

processed nonfood
food
n/a substance

frozen   dry products

deli

bakery

alcohol   checkout

produce

candy

► Participant 1
31 items total =
17 food +
14 sad nonfood

► Participant 2
13 items total =
7 food +
6 sad nonfood

► Participant 3
40 items total =
16 food +
34 sad nonfood

Behavioral mapping of consumer routes in a grocery store are combined with shadowing observations and conversation to establish a picture of shopping patterns.

Bodystorming

Brainstorming and spontaneous prototyping
through dynamic physical experience and role-play

- Designers immerse themselves in user situations
  through simulated contexts while paying close
  attention to decisions, interactive experiences, and
  emotional responses.

- Concept ideas can be integrated and tested in play,
  and the active situation can inspire the spontaneous
  creation of new product and service concepts.

- Bodystorming prototypes use simple constructions
  and props at hand: for example, cardboard, boxes,
  existing objects, furniture, and lighting manipulations.

- While scenarios may be partially scripted from
  observations, the bodystorm encourages
  improvisation to capture real-world experiences.

- The method may be contained within design teams
  but can also engage a wider audience of peers or
  clients, inviting response and dialogue.

See also   Experience Prototyping • Role-Playing •
Simulation Exercises

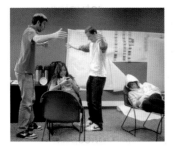

Designers bodystorm an alarm system with personal bubbles of sound space controlled by mobile devices, awakening one person while a roommate continues to sleep.

Brainstorm Graphic Organizers

Visual structures of new ideas and concepts

- Brainstorming creates a judgment-free zone to express creative ideas and explore new concepts.

- Widely accepted rules include, "quantity over quality," "withhold judgment and criticism," "build on each other's ideas," and "welcome oddity."

- Graphic organizers, or visual representations of knowledge, are sense-making frameworks that facilitate teams as they brainstorm unconventional alternatives within a domain.

- **Brainstorming Webs** help develop a central concept or question, identifying its characteristics, supporting facts, and related ideas.

- **Tree Diagrams** communicate hierarchy, a classification system, or relationships between main and supporting ideas.

- **Flow Diagrams** document a sequence of events, represent the actions or processes of different actors in a system, or show cause and effect of interrelated elements.

See also   Cognitive Mapping • Concept Mapping • Mind Mapping

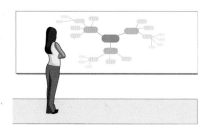

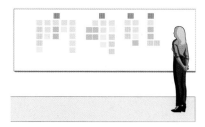

Webs, Trees, and Flow Diagrams provide sense-making frameworks for facilitating and visualizing brainstorming, disrupting and challenging old patterns of thinking.

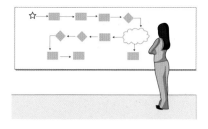

Business Origami

Paper-prototyping interactions and value exchanges among people, artifacts, and environments

- Business origami is a service design activity where stakeholders build a physical representation of a system and then prototype future or alternative states.

- Paper tokens represent actors, artifacts, environments, and technologies on a horizontal whiteboard "stage" where interactions play out to tell a story.

- Lines and arrows labeled on the whiteboard represent the interactions between tokens, articulating what value people get out of the exchange.

- The method gives all participants an equal voice in the prototyping activity, bridging different perspectives by providing a common reference for further discussion.

- The experience of physical modeling is critical, making the value exchange explicit within a scenario.

See also   Creative Toolkits • Design Workshops • User Journey Maps

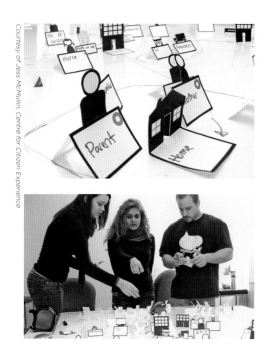

Paper pop-up "origami" tokens represent people, locations, artifacts, technology, transportation, channels, third parties, social media, and proprietary tools, with lines and arrows illustrating relationships.

Card Sorting

Participant sorting of concepts, terms, or features into meaningful categories and relationships using printed cards

- Used to explore how participants group items into categories and relate concepts to one another, whether for digital interface design or a table of contents.

- It can be used to identify terminology that is vague, misunderstood, or has multiple meanings associated with it.

- Card sorting can also be used to generate options for structuring information, identifying different schemas for organizing navigation, menus, and taxonomies.

- It validates that the categories in your product or service actually reflect the mental model of your audience.

- Including blank cards and markers allows participants to add their own items where needed.

- If no consistent patterns emerge after several card sorts, consider renaming the cards or reconsider the categories.

See also   Automated Remote Research •
Content Inventory & Audit • Desirability Testing

Card sorting can help you understand how people group information, perceive and describe different groups of information, and generate ideas for navigation categories.

Case Studies

In-depth investigation of single instances to gain detailed knowledge using multiple sources

- This is useful for understanding existing phenomena for comparison or inspiration and to study the effects of change, new programs, or innovations.

- Instances, or cases, may be of individuals, events, organizations, entire communities, or processes.

- Details of cases emerge during data collection and analysis, which typically include the following features:

  - Selection of a case or small set of cases

  - Study of the case in its social and physical context

  - Collection of information using multiple, triangulated methods such as interviews, observations, unobtrusive trace measures, and document analysis

- This method welcomes extraordinary cases and outliers rather than looking for representative instances.

- Similar to the design process, case studies require the researcher to determine a problem, make hypotheses, conduct research, revise theory, and tell a story.

See also Evidence-Based Design • Research Through Design • Secondary Research

When well composed and designed, case studies can result in compelling human narratives, with vivid details that make the case more memorable.

Cognitive Mapping

A visualization technique that reveals how people process and make sense of their experience

- Cognitive maps are most effective when used to structure complex problems.
- It's designed specifically as a decision-making tool that can inform strategic direction.
- Unlike concept maps or mind maps, the format and structure require no central focus of visualization.
- Nodes of a cognitive map are made up of the exact words and phrases spoken by participants.
- Each node can have as many incoming and outgoing associations as necessary and are read as causal pathways: for example, *node x may imply node y*.
- Cognitive mapping can facilitate the note-taking process during interviews and when transcribing text-based qualitative data.

See also   Content Analysis • Concept Mapping •
Mind Mapping

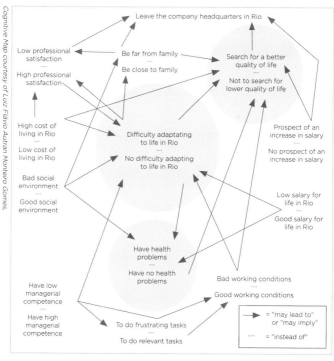

In the figure:

Leave the company headquarters in Rio

Low professional satisfaction
....
High professional satisfaction

Be far from family
....
Be close to family

Search for a better quality of life
....
Not to search for lower quality of life

High cost of living in Rio
....
Low cost of living in Rio

Difficulty adapting to life in Rio
....
No difficulty adapting to life in Rio

Prospect of an increase in salary
....
No prospect of an increase in salary

Bad social environment
....
Good social environment

Low salary for life in Rio
....
Good salary for life in Rio

Have health problems
....
Have no health problems

Have low managerial competence
....
Have high managerial competence

Bad working conditions
....
Good working conditions

To do frustrating tasks
....
To do relevant tasks

= "may lead to" or "may imply"

.... = "instead of"

Cognitive maps reveal people's underlying agendas and decision-making criteria. This map is based on a questionnaire for employees considering leaving a company headquarters.

Cognitive Walkthrough

Evaluating whether the order of prompts in a system reflects the way people cognitively process tasks

- This is a usability inspection method that evaluates a system's anticipated ease-of-use without instruction, coaching, or training.

- Each step of the interaction with the system can be assessed as a step that either moves the individual closer to or further from their goal.

- Evaluators ask four questions for each step in the sequence:

  1. Will users want to produce whatever effect the action has?

  2. Will users see the control (button, menu, label, etc.) for the action?

  3. Will users recognize that the control will produce the effect that they want?

  4. Will users understand feedback they get, so they can confidently continue on to the next action?

- It should be used with usability testing to uncover different classes of design issues and problems.

See also   Heuristic Evaluation • Think-Aloud Protocol • Wizard of Oz

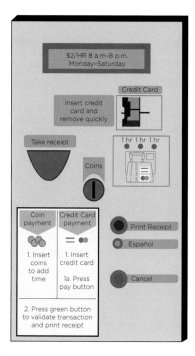

Cognitive walkthroughs are used to evaluate whether an interface is understandable and easy to learn based on the user's problem-solving mental operations.

Collage

The visual expression of thoughts, feelings, desires, and other aspects of life using images and words

- It can help mitigate the limitations of traditional verbal means in gathering innermost thoughts.

- The paper canvas may be blank, or it may have lines to suggest placement such as past, present, and ideal future.

- Collage kits should have images and words ambiguous enough to avoid bias, yet specific enough to be relevant.

- Blank frames or stickers and markers should be included for participants to add their own material.

- A single person usually completes a collage, but sessions are generally conducted in small groups.

- Participants present their collages to the group, providing insight about choices for analysis.

- Qualitative analysis is used to look for patterns and themes within and across several collages, such as use or non-use of elements, placement, and relationship.

See also   Creative Toolkits • Generative Research • Participatory Design

Collage allows participants to project their thoughts, feelings, and desires onto a visual artifact, providing insight and inspiration for design teams.

Competitive Testing

Research to evaluate the usability and learnability of your competitors' products

- This complements traditional marketing strategies and business audits by considering the social, economic, and technical context.

- It allows design teams to assess a competitor's products from the end user's point of view.

- Teams inspect how usable and learnable competitors' digital applications are by conducting usability tests on competitive products, as well as on their own.

- In contrast to attitudinal surveys, competitive testing focuses on end-user behavior as people attempt to accomplish tasks that exist across products.

- By understanding key similarities and differences between competitors, gaps can be identified for further market differentiation or specialization.

- Results from competitive tests should be ongoing, tracked, and compared over time.

See also   Kano Analysis • Think-Aloud Protocol • Value Opportunity Analysis

Before designing a shopping assistant for a retail warehouse
environment, a design team conducted competitive research of
existing, in-store help kiosks.

Concept Mapping

A visual framework connecting a large number of ideas, objects, and events as they relate to a certain domain

- This provides scaffolding that can help visualize the complexities of a system to make new meaning.

- Concept maps consist of individual concepts (a well-understood idea, object, or event; usually nouns connected by linking words (usually verbs).

- Linking words that connect two or more concepts form a proposition that creates a meaningful statement.

- Articulating the correct focus question is a key step that will provide context and structure to the map.

- After a focus question is generated, a list of fifteen to twenty-five concepts should be identified and ranked from general to very specific.

- A preliminary map is constructed and then revised until a final map emerges to adequately answer the focus questions.

- Maps should help design teams gain new knowledge and find new meanings in an information space.

See also Brainstorm Graphic Organizers • Cognitive Mapping • Mind Mapping

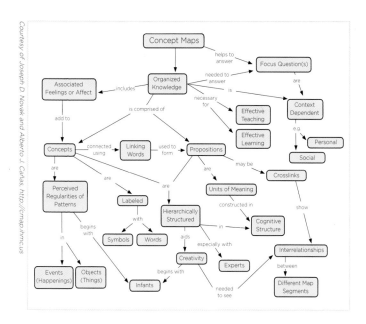

Concept maps are organized in a downward hierarchy, with the focus question at the top of the map and the most general concepts below it.

Content Analysis

The systematic description of form and content of written, spoken, or visual materials expressed in themes, patterns, and counts

- Content analysis provides an established and systematic technique for dealing with qualitative data.

- In inductive content analysis, the categories or codes are derived from a systematic reading of a sample set of the materials to be analyzed.

- In deductive content analysis, codes or categories are derived beforehand, often based on a theoretical framework.

- Content analysis can identify themes and patterns in the data, including how dominantly they are represented.

- Outcomes can be quantitative, counting occurrences of the words, phrases, images, or concepts.

- The method also examines form and structure of communication: for example, scale and location of images or the font and type size of text.

- For smaller sample sets, content analysis can be done manually; for larger sets, software is available.

See also Affinity Diagramming • Thematic Networks • Word Clouds

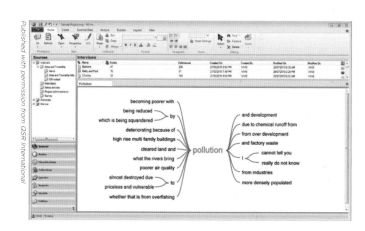

Content analysis helps you extract themes and make meaning out of unstructured information, often with the help of software. *Shown: Word tree from NVivo 9.*

Content Inventory & Audit

A content inventory tells you what your content is;
an audit recommends what it should be

- Everything a customer can read, watch, interact with,
  or listen to can be considered content.

- Perform an inventory and audit:

  - When beginning a website redesign

  - When merging multiple sites or splitting up into
    smaller, niche sites

  - When preparing content for multichannel
    distribution or a Content Management System (CMS)

- A content inventory organizes assets into a
  spreadsheet of content items and attributes.

- A quantitative content audit assesses the attributes of
  "Governance," including ownership, copyright, and
  creative details.

- The qualitative content audit rates "Content Quality"
  criteria such as credibility, originality, accuracy, and
  relevance to identify unifying themes and patterns
  across content sources.

See also Card Sorting • Key Performance Indicators •
Site Search Analytics

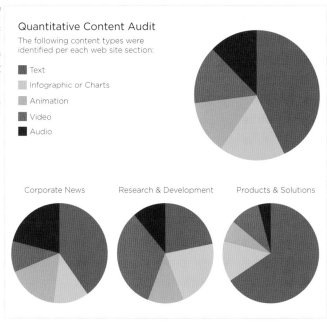

Quantitative Content Audit

The following content types were
identified per each web site section:

- Text
- Infographic or Charts
- Animation
- Video
- Audio

Corporate News   Research & Development   Products & Solutions

Content inventories and audits can provide quantitative and
qualitative visualizations to help stakeholders understand
where content stands and where it needs to be.

Contextual Design

A customer-centered process that makes designer workflow concrete, explicit, and sharable

- Designers intuitively understand the leap from customer-centered data to a sound design direction, but to non-designers this process can seem "fuzzy" or "magic."

- Recommended steps to make design work more predictable and inclusive of non-designers include:

  - *Contextual Inquiry* to understand the customer

  - *Interpretation Sessions* for each customer interview

  - *Work Models and Affinity Diagrams* to represent the complex systems of work

  - *Visioning and Storyboarding* to generate concepts to support the customer's work

  - *User Environment Design* to document natural flow of the customer's work

  - *Paper Mock-ups* to get feedback from customers before coding and implementation

- The process can reduce the time it takes to move through customer-centered design challenges.

See also Affinity Diagramming • Contextual Inquiry • Storyboards

Contextual Design process steps

Requirements & Solutions	Contextual Inquiry	Talk to specific customers in the field	1
	Interpretation Session	Interpret the data as a team to capture issues	
	Work Models & Affinity Diagramming	Consolidate data across customers for a full market view	
	Visioning	Redesign people's work with new technology ideas	2
Define & Validate Concepts	Storyboarding	Work out the details of particular tasks and roles	
	User Environment Design	Design system to support this work	3
	Paper Mock-Up Interviews	Mock up the interface using interaction patterns for testing	
	Interaction & Visual Design	Design and test the final look and user experience	4

Contextual design is a customer-centered process that begins with data from contextual inquiry, intended to help with transitions between common steps of the design process.

Contextual Inquiry

An immersive, contextual way to observe and interview that reveals underlying work structure

- Four principles define the contextual inquiry method:

  1. **Context:** To understand the ongoing experience and tacit knowledge of the worker, it is critical that the researcher observe details in context.

  2. **Partnership:** This is similar to a master/apprentice model, watching, asking questions, and seeking to understand how the data more reliably reflects reality.

  3. **Interpretation:** What researchers see and hear must be interpreted for meaning and double-checked with participants on-site.

  4. **Focus:** The researcher must learn to expand beyond personal focus to see more in the participant's world, picking up on idiosyncrasies and contradictions.

- This is used to understand communication flows, sequence of tasks, artifacts, tools, and the influence of culture and the physical environment on work.

- Interview multiple people in different user segments before synthesizing contextual inquiry findings.

See also Affinity Diagramming • Contextual Design • Interviews

Contextual Inquiry provides a way to structure interviews with people that reveal specific details about how they work and helps expose underlying work structure.

Creative Toolkits

Collections of physical elements organized for participatory modeling, visualization, or creative play

- Facilitated participatory exercises can provide people with a tangible artifact on which to project thoughts, feelings, desires, and emotions.

- Flexible or Velcro modeling kits contain a range of three-dimensional forms, buttons, and ambiguous design elements that can be easily configured.

- Interface kits can contain paper or card elements representing design features for flexible arrangement, suggesting mock or ideal web or device interactions.

- Collage kits can contain an inventory of images and words or shape and symbol elements for open interpretation and use relevant to the design inquiry.

- Drawing kits will contain various papers, cards, and writing tools accommodating a range of potential exercises.

- Depending on the intent of the exercise, kits can be built from original materials or from existing parts, toys, or games.

See also   Design Workshops • Generative Research • Participatory Design

Here is a typical Velcro modeling kit with form and element variations designed for physical manipulation and configuration by participants.

Critical Incident Technique

Understanding how users experience your product at critical moments to optimize future designs

- Ask individuals to describe a situation with your product or service.
- Collect positive and negative experiences through directed storytelling, interviews, or diary studies to identify:
  - *The incident cause:* What were the events leading up to the critical incident?
  - *User actions:* What were the behaviors that took place during the incident?
  - *User sentiment:* How did the user feel during the incident and afterward?
  - *Incident outcome:* Did the user change how he or she behaved after the incident?
  - *Ideal outcome:* What are possible future outcomes?
- Representative scenarios cover possible explanations and recommendations.
- Prioritize and triangulate with other research to gain a better understanding of situations that have a profound impact on user behavior.

See also   Diary Studies • Directed Storytelling • Interviews

The Critical Incident Technique focuses on how people solve problems, with the goal of optimizing and recreating successful results and eliminating the negative, counterproductive ones.

Crowdsourcing

Voluntary completion of tasks or micro-projects by an undefined, large group of people

- This brings together users and testers to evaluate prototypes and submit potential solutions to problems.

- Micro-tasks are accessed via a common platform that can be completed by volunteers within seconds or minutes.

- Participants receive monetary (a micropayment) or nonmonetary (reputation points) compensation.

- Design straightforward, uncomplicated tasks to get the most volunteers to participate.

- Include questions that have a bona-fide answer as part of the task to prevent volunteers from "gaming" the system by entering nonsense responses.

- Devise tasks so that completing them correctly and in good faith requires as much or even less work than entering random, invalid responses.

- Consider triangulation with other methods to increase confidence of research outcomes.

See also   Automated Remote Research • Photo Studies • Triangulation

Using crowdsourcing, frog design's frogMob invites people from all over the world to upload their photographs of interesting trends to inform and inspire designers.

Cultural Probes

Provocative instruments to inspire new forms of self-understanding and communication

- Use materials such as postcards, journals, cameras, text, and imagery to gather personal insights from participants.

- Provocations are designed to inspire people to thoughtfully consider personal context and circumstance and respond in unique, creative ways.

- Materials should be varied and imaginative to elicit responses that are relevant to the design inquiry.

- Probes are flexible, open-ended, and intentionally subjective, collecting inspirational data to stimulate design imagination.

- Design probes support empathic understanding through information gathering over a prolonged period, where the researcher cannot be present.

- Probe kits are combined with other research methods such as observations, site visits, and interviews.

- Probes should be thoughtful in aesthetic craft, message, and delivery and be created to inspire delight and respect, response, and return.

See also Diary Studies • Experience Sampling Method • Photo Studies

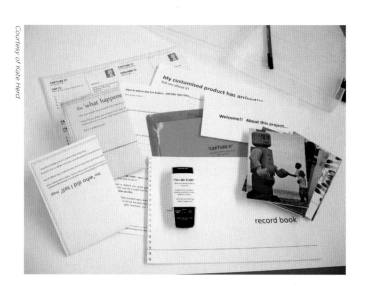

A study on mass-customization of products collected personal stories of participants using a cultural probe kit of digital voice recorders, cameras, postcards, diaries, and stickers.

Customer Experience Audit

Capturing the day-to-day context in which people engage with your product or service

- This captures what customers do, think, and use as they set out to achieve a goal that involves your product or service.

- It provides a framework that design teams can use to isolate specific moments of delight, apathy, or frustration before, during, and after an experience.

- Individual moments can be transformed into sources of design team inspiration, from which opportunities for innovation can be identified.

- Qualitative data from interviews and directed storytelling reflects people's social, environmental, and financial realities, underlying beliefs, values, and desires.

- Experience audits can help researchers isolate the areas where they may need to conduct more research as well as any gaps in the service or product offering.

- To keep up with changing social, economic, and technical factors, the audit should be repeated to assess experience with your product over time.

See also   Diary Studies • Directed Storytelling • Experience Sampling Method

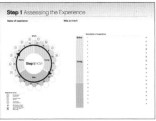

As part of every experience design project at the LEGO Group, audits help designers assess whether intended experiences live up to user perceptions and expectations.

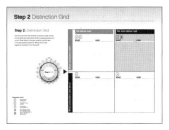

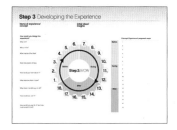

Design Charette

A workshop-style technique providing sequential rounds of collaboration and cross-pollination of design ideas

- Designers and non-designers—including project stakeholders, engineers, and users—can participate.
- Participants rapidly generate ideas and rotate through small groups to bring forward the best ideas and move toward superior design concepts.
- This can be used to explore ideas for large-scale design challenges or generate possibilities regarding a very specific interface.
- A moderator should communicate that each round of designs builds off the preferred components identified in the prior cycle.
- The sessions should be low-tech, using basic tools, paper templates, pencils, erasers, and color markers.
- Clarity can be achieved through the active comparison and contrast of many ideas.

See also   Design Workshops • Parallel Prototyping • Participatory Design

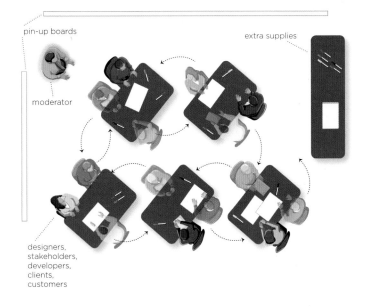

pin-up boards

extra supplies

moderator

designers,
stakeholders,
developers,
clients,
customers

Designers, stakeholders, and developers rapidly generate
ideas, rotating through small groups to bring forward and
cross-pollinate the best ideas and move toward superior
design concepts.

Design Ethnography

Deep immersive experience and understanding of a user's world for design empathy and insight

- This is characterized by descriptive accounts of people in their natural settings, typically using qualitative methods.

- It is focused on a highly contextual, comprehensive, and empathic understanding of users, their lives, their language, their artifacts, and their behaviors.

- In contrast to anthropologist ethnographers who immerse themselves in a culture over extensive periods of time, designers aim to sample behaviors.

- Common methods include experience sampling, diary and photo studies, cultural probes, contextual inquiry, conversational interviews, touchstone tours, and observations.

- Analysis is based on deciphering patterns and themes articulated in a set of design implications in preparation for generative research.

See also Cultural Probes • Exploratory Research • Participant Observation

Design ethnography is performed on the mechanic's garage, from a study of understanding how technical knowledge and preventative car care might be supported through design.

028

Design Workshops

Creative work sessions with participants organized around codesign methods

- Gain the creative trust and input of stakeholders and secure buy-in from team members and clients.

- Workshops can consist of projective techniques such as collage, mapping, or diagramming, to gain an understanding of the user's world.

- There are common in generative research, with participants contributing to ideation through codesign.

- In evaluative sessions, participants collectively review concepts, offer feedback, and contribute insights for design iteration and refinement.

- Workshops may include hands-on training of simple design tools, enabling participants to create mock-ups, sketches, or storyboards, or role-play interactions.

- Plan carefully for a balance of design team facilitators relative to the number of participants, with clearly defined roles.

- These workshops are increasingly used to train interested non-design audiences in the common methods of design research, ideation, thinking, and processes.

See also   Creative Toolkits • Generative Research • Participatory Design

Design workshops engage participants, often non-designers, in intense creative activity centered on assigned problems, as in this workshop on design thinking for business executives.

029

Desirability Testing

Gauging first-impression emotional responses to product and service designs

- This explores the affective response that different designs elicit from people based on first impressions.

- Using index cards with positive, neutral, and negative adjectives written on them, participants pick those that describe how they feel about a design or prototype.

- It can focus attention on responses from end users, instead of on personal opinions that often leave teams at an impasse.

- When the process is applied repeatedly, the team can begin to compare and cluster the words that are most frequently chosen and visualize the results.

- The method helps focus the design team efforts on shaping the exact emotional response they want people to have while using their products.

- It Can be conducted using low-fidelity prototypes or on products already in the public domain as a baseline before the team embarks on a redesign.

See also   Triangulation • Usability Testing •
Value Opportunity Analysis

Microsoft Product Reaction Cards are a powerful tool for gathering emotional feedback.

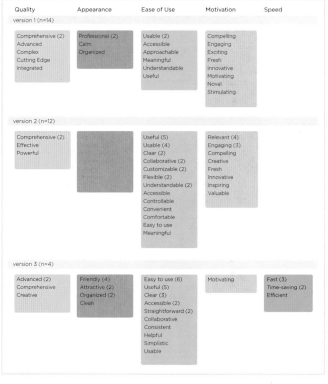

Quality	Appearance	Ease of Use	Motivation	Speed

version 1 (n=14)

Quality	Appearance	Ease of Use	Motivation	Speed
Comprehensive (2)	Professional (2)	Usable (2)	Compelling	
Advanced	Calm	Accessible	Engaging	
Complex	Organized	Approachable	Exciting	
Cutting Edge		Meaningful	Fresh	
Integrated		Understandable	Innovative	
		Useful	Motivating	
			Novel	
			Stimulating	

version 2 (n=12)

Quality	Appearance	Ease of Use	Motivation	Speed
Comprehensive (2)		Useful (5)	Relevant (4)	
Effective		Usable (4)	Engaging (3)	
Powerful		Clear (2)	Compelling	
		Collaborative (2)	Creative	
		Customizable (2)	Fresh	
		Flexible (2)	Innovative	
		Understandable (2)	Inspiring	
		Accessible	Valuable	
		Controllable		
		Convenient		
		Comfortable		
		Easy to use		
		Meaningful		

version 3 (n=4)

Quality	Appearance	Ease of Use	Motivation	Speed
Advanced (2)	Friendly (4)	Easy to use (6)	Motivating	Fast (3)
Comprehensive	Attractive (2)	Useful (5)		Time-saving (2)
Creative	Organized (2)	Clear (3)		Efficient
	Clean	Accessible (2)		
		Straightforward (2)		
		Collaborative		
		Consistent		
		Helpful		
		Simplistic		
		Usable		

030

Diary Studies

Guiding journals for convenient expression of personal details about daily life and events

- They are ideal for collecting thoughts, feelings, or behaviors from participants at key moments across time.

- They are designed for portability and ease of use, with an overview of the topic instructions and a sample entry.

- Participants may be requested to document each time they engage in a particular behavior, encounter a product or situation, or have specific interactions.

- Creative page formats can be used to invite text entries, sketches, drawings, photographs, or stickers and multiple-choice responses.

- In rare cases, diaries may be used for usability studies or evaluation, as a means of collecting feedback from users testing products in context over time.

- Using digital diaries, participants record entries on mobile devices or via email or web-based uploads.

See also   Cultural Probes • Experience Sampling Method • Photo Studies

(top) Traditional diary study on skincare regimens conducted using pen-and-paper journals. **(bottom)** Digital diary with user photo and text entries describing Christmas shopping experiences.

031

Directed Storytelling

Gathering rich stories of lived experiences using narrative conversational prompts

- This is rooted in narrative inquiry, whereby researchers understand people and document their experiences from personal stories.

- It starts with a prompt by the researcher to the storyteller: "Tell me a story about the last time you . . ."

- Additional guiding questions are posed in terms of who, what, when, where, and how, to keep the storyteller in a comfortable narrative flow.

- Ideas emerging from stories can be clustered using affinity diagramming, looking for consistent patterns and themes within and across experiences.

- Themes that characterize experiences can be modeled into a tangible framework, with maps or diagrams of what is most significant about participant experiences.

- The method may provide subtle reinforcement and validation of existing design directions or identify the need for additional research.

See also   Interviews • Critical Incident Technique • Picture Cards

Guiding questions for directed storytelling might include the following: When and with whom did you interact? What aspects of the environment affected your experience? How did you feel?

032

Elito Method

A method used to ground design arguments in research observations and business directives

- This is a rigorous synthesis method designed to help teams bridge the "analysis-synthesis" gap between research and design ideas in a business context.

- Elito brings the multidisciplinary team together after primary and/or secondary research has been conducted.

- Using a spreadsheet and a projector, the team captures its work and thinking in five "Elito entities," which together create "logic line" design arguments:

  - *Observation*: "What did you see, read, or hear?"

  - *Judgment*: "What is your opinion about that observation?"

  - *Value*: "What values are ultimately at work?"

  - *Concept/Sketch*: "What can the design team do to solve this problem?"

  - *Key Metaphor*: "What is the hook or tagline?"

- The spreadsheet captures the team's random, nonlinear thinking to connect arguments, further refine ideas, and organize arguments into observation-based themes.

See also Cultural Probes • Design Ethnography • Touchstone Tours

After building an Elito spreadsheet based on research observations, each "logic line" is sorted, clustered, and commented upon to analyze, evaluate, and share the work.

033

Ergonomic Analysis

An assessment of tools, devices, or environments to optimize fit, safety, and comfort

- Performed to suggest redesign improvements or establish ergonomic criteria for new design.
- The five interrelated criteria commonly used are:
  1. **Size:** Anthropometry is the systematic measurement of people to assess and design tools and systems.
  2. **Strength:** Manual force encompasses finger/hand strength for triggering and gripping and body strength for lifting.
  3. **Reach:** Assesses safe access to operator controls or environmental features and is typically based on fifth percentile females to accommodate most users.
  4. **Clearance:** Assesses effective space within and around machinery and for avoiding environmental obstacles and is commonly based on the 95th percentile male.
  5. **Posture:** Tool and system design should avoid excessive hand deviation or flexion and the reduction of bending and stooping to avoid discomfort, fatigue, and long-term injury.

See also Evaluative Research • Task Analysis • Usability Testing

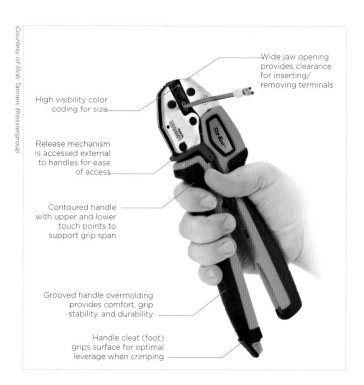

Wide jaw opening
provides clearance
for inserting/
removing terminals

High visibility color
coding for size

Release mechanism
is accessed external
to handles for ease
of access

Contoured handle
with upper and lower
touch points to
support grip span

Grooved handle overmolding
provides comfort, grip
stability, and durability

Handle cleat (foot)
grips surface for optimal
leverage when crimping

An ergonomic analysis of a crimping device hand tool for
Thomas & Betts.

034

Evaluative Research

Testing of prototypes, products, or interfaces by users of a system in design development

- This gauges human expectations against a designed artifact, determining whether something is useful, usable, and desirable.

- Testing should collect performance measures such as task speed and accuracy and preference measures such as aesthetic and emotional response.

- Research of existing and competing products may be useful in early stage design research, to inform new product development.

- Testing may be conducted in a lab setting or by people using products or prototypes in a real-world context.

- New crowdsourcing opportunities afford online testing by volunteers to assess how users are engaging with prototype interface designs and wireframes.

- Some forms of evaluation research such as cognitive walkthrough and heuristic evaluation use expert evaluators to assess products and interfaces.

See also A/B Testing • Heuristic Evaluation • Think-Aloud Protocol

Evaluation research can be formal or informal. In this example, evaluations were invited through a public display of prototypes for a proposed new signage program.

035

Evidence-Based Design

Effective design decisions based on credible research and assessed outcomes

- Evidence-Based Design (EBD) and Evidence-Based Research connect evidence and application, or the applied use of known theories validated by research.

- EBD is applicable across the spectrum of design disciplines for improving service and product touch-points within any environment.

- The primary tenets of EBD are to enter the problem unbiased, employing traditional research methods and factual evidence to influence design decision-making.

- Methods include credible literature reviews and comparative analyses, case studies, and documented post-use evaluations of existing design.

- EBD should also include documented site visits, surveys, interviews, and other means of collecting information.

- Design decisions should be linked to measurable outcomes to justify return on investment, such as reduced infection rates or decreased staff injuries.

See also   Case Studies • Literature Reviews • Secondary Research

This material is based upon work supported by the National Science Foundation under Grant No. IIS-0325047. Courtesy of Peter Scupelli.

Figure 1. An existing surgical suite control desk and schedule board.

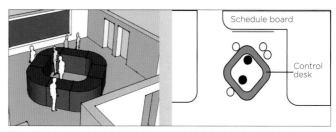

Figure 2. Three dimensional sketch of new control desk and schedule board. New floor plan of same. Black circles are control desk workers: white circles are information seekers.

An Evidence-Based Design of a surgical suite requires that research informs design decisions, hypotheses are linked to outcomes, design is evaluated, and results are published.

036

Experience Prototyping

Active participation in design through subjective engagement with a prototype system or service, product, or place

- Similar to role-playing and bodystorming, low-fidelity prototypes or props are used to help create a realistic scenario of use and activate felt experiences.

- For exploring and evaluating ideas, design teams can use this method internally and with clients and users.

- Prototypes may include simple props and role-playing or physical and digital prototypes with some level of functionality tested in realistic situations.

- Experience prototyping is effective for persuading key audiences of the values inherent in design concepts, through direct and active engagement.

- A level of functionality allows realistic engagement, yet with a caution that the prototype represents a work in progress and not the final design artifact.

- Advantages are a low cost and addressing situations that will prevent real-life experiences because of inherent risks and dangers or complicating logistics.

See also   Bodystorming • Role-Playing • Wizard of Oz

Experience prototypes surround a prototype product or service with a simulated context of use. Here, a user schedules an appointment using a mobile device prototype.

037

Experience Sampling Method

Behaviors, interactions, thoughts, or feelings self-reported in real time when signaled

- Experience sampling requires participants to document something specific when signaled by a device alarm.

- Before smartphones, participants were signaled by pagers, hence the common nickname of "beeper study."

- Behaviors, interactions, thoughts, or feelings are guided by clear instructions and entered into a pre-established form, often with photos in a diary or journal.

- Technology allows for documenting and sending photos, text, or audio entries through smartphones.

- This is a form of design ethnography, collecting strategic samples of life in place of in-person immersion by researchers.

- Samples can give the designer a comprehensive picture across time or individuals for any particular design study.

- The method is useful in exploratory and generative phases of design research.

See also   Design Ethnography • Diary Studies • Photo Studies

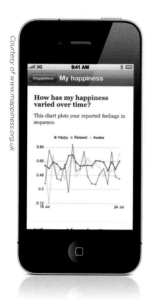

The "Mappiness" project uses experience sampling to invite respondents to indicate their current feelings and situation when paged, mapping how the environment affects people's happiness.

038

Experiments

Measuring the effect that an action has on a situation, demonstrating a causal relationship

- Cause and effect criteria are met by the cause occurring before the effect of two observable and measurable actions or events and elimination of all other possible causes.

- Through random assignment, experimental group participants are exposed to manipulations of an independent variable, while the control group is not.

- All other conditions are held exactly the same for both groups to rule out the influence of extraneous variables.

- The dependent variable is measured to see if there is a significant difference for those exposed to the manipulation.

- An operational definition defines exactly how the dependent variable is being measured: for example, performance speed or assessment of comfort.

- Quasi-experiments occur when the researcher cannot control the assignment of participants to conditions: for example, comparing pre-existing groups.

See also A/B Testing • Evaluative Research • Eyetracking

In a vision experiment, people were equally good at categorizing the gist of briefly glimpsed scenes using peripheral vision as when seeing the entire image.

039

Exploratory Research

User and product studies intended to forge an empathic knowledge base

- Conducted in the early stages of the design process and set by the planning, scoping, and definition phase.

- The focus is on gaining a solid knowledge base of the design territory and existing artifacts and forging an empathic sense of the people targeted by the design.

- A variety of diverse yet complementary methods might include contextual inquiry, touchstone tours, surveys, observation, experience sampling, and cultural probes.

- Research is purposefully flexible, encouraging divergence from planned protocols and the inclusion of data from spontaneous interactions and observations.

- Synthesis is critical, but targeted toward inspiration rather than the formal analysis of concrete data.

- Exploratory research culminates in a set of tangible design implications, preparing the groundwork for generative research and concept development.

See also   Cultural Probes • Design Ethnography • Observation

Exploratory research for a service design project on meat purchasing behaviors included surveys, farm visits, observations, and conversations at meat counters with butchers and consumers.

040

Eyetracking

Technical information documenting where and f
or how long people are looking when using an
interface or interacting with products

- Eye movements tracked during reading or image-gaze
  tasks are identified for moments of fixation and rapid
  movements from point to point between fixations.

- Technology traces and documents patterns, generating
  data for interface and design usability studies.

- Optical methods are used to capture corneal reflections
  of infrared light on video using sophisticated cameras.
  Small sensing electrodes precisely detect movements.

- It can help examine printed text and visual materials,
  engaging with products or product assembly tasks,
  and navigating environments.

- Data is used to generate heat maps, aggregating data
  from several participants for a visual analysis of scan
  patterns and distributed attention.

- Eyetracking should be triangulated with other research
  methods to understand user motivations, information
  processing, or comprehension.

See also Automated Remote Research • Experiments •
Evaluative Research

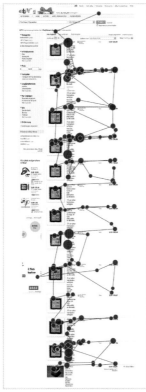

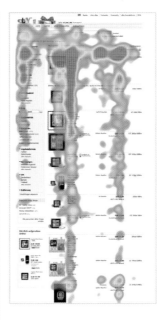

Eyetracking and heat maps are used by eBay to understand where ads could be most effective and useful, helping to shape an advertising strategy.

041

Flexible Modeling

Product or interface configurations generated by users from a component kit of parts

- In industrial design, Velcro modeling presents physical product forms and features sets such as buttons and controls covered in fabric and fasteners for quick configurations.

- In interaction design, interface elements may be presented on paper, card, or in digital form for the users to arrange in a way that makes sense to them.

- For environmental design and space planning, scale model parts or paper templates can be arranged.

- Ambiguous elements may be configured to represent either realistic or ideal "fantasy" artifacts for participants to overlay their own expressions, needs, and desires.

- For analysis, configured artifacts can be sorted by similar characteristics, common user choices, or themes.

- Resulting models can be visually translated into refined designs, using the information provided by participants as guiding inspiration for the designer.

See also Creative Toolkits • Generative Research • Participatory Design

Flexible modeling presents the participant with a kit of
ambiguous parts, in this case components of a backpack, to be
configured into preferred arrangements.

042

Fly-on-the-Wall Observation

Unobtrusive observation of people or behaviors, without direct participation or interference

- This method attempts to minimize potential bias or behavioral influences that might result from engagement with users.

- It is appropriate when observing public behaviors or work processes that may be unduly influenced if interrupted or inconvenienced.

- It may reduce the researcher's ability to connect empathically with people and probe further into motivations behind participant behaviors.

- It is generally conducted flexibly, although worksheets or other guiding frameworks may usefully inform observations.

- *Secret outsiders* are distant observers, with a vantage point that removes them from participants to minimize any influence on behaviors.

- *Recognized outsiders* have the nature of their research and role as observer made known to participants, but position themselves in a natural and unobtrusive way.

See also   Observation • Shadowing • Unobtrusive Measures

Fly-on-the-Wall Observation is an ideal method for studying public places and activities.

043

Focus Groups

Gauging opinions, feelings, and attitudes about a product, service, marketing campaign, or brand

- The dynamic created by a small group of carefully recruited people, when guided by a skilled moderator, can provide insight into themes, patterns, and trends.

- Allows participants to openly share experiences, perceptions, wants/needs, and fantasies.

- Design-related inquiries may include:

  - Reviewing processes that take place over time

  - Explanations of what is not desirable about the current state

  - Uncovering the underlying emotions while going through a given process

  - Work-arounds and hacks to improve the process

  - Learning how members establish social capital

  - Understanding constructs and mental models shared by group members

- Pay attention to the logic behind conclusions, stories, metaphors, and analogies, as well as how participants describe their experiences, preferences, and memories.

See also   Directed Storytelling • Laddering • Surveys

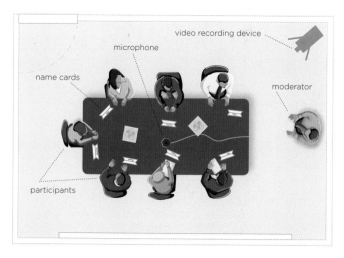

video recording device

microphone

name cards

moderator

participants

A skilled moderator guides a focus group. Sessions are commonly recorded, or stakeholders may observe the session through one-way glass or on screen.

044

Generative Research

Engaging users in creative activities to provide rich information for concept development

- Participatory methods include codesign activities as a collaborative process between user and designer.

- Methods may include creative tool kits, design workshops, card sorting, collages, cognitive mapping, diagramming, drawing, and flexible modeling.

- The creation of an artifact around which a participant may talk will act as a trigger for engaged conversation.

- Early phase expressive exercises such as collage enable participants to articulate feelings and desires.

- Later phase exercises consist of constructive methods such as flexible modeling, manipulating design elements oriented toward concept generation.

- Participatory exercises are combined with verbal discussions of work in progress and presentations of creative artifacts emerging from research sessions.

- Focus is on the generation of design concepts and early prototype iterations, ultimately preparing for evaluation, refinement, and production.

See also   Creative Toolkits • Flexible Modeling • Participatory Design

Flexible modeling kits are used by participants in constructive
generative research. Here, they are being used to propose
desired elements for smartphone apps.

045

Graffiti Walls

An open canvas inviting comments about an environment or system in the context of use

- Large-format paper is temporarily adhered to a wall, with markers readily available for posting open-ended comments.

- The paper may be blank, or a guiding question may be posed to maintain a particular theme.

- The method is useful in environments or situations where it is challenging to collect information through traditional methods such as interview or observation.

- Photos of each graffiti wall should be taken at daily intervals, as the paper may deteriorate or be removed.

- The graffiti wall can be analyzed as a research artifact, for inspiration, comparison, consolidation with walls collected from other locations, and content analysis.

- One limitation is the lack of control and knowledge about who contributed to the information and why.

See also   Exploratory Research • Observation • Unobtrusive Measures

Graffiti walls are ideal for capturing informal opinions about an environment in the context of use, seen here for research on attitudes about public bathrooms.

046

Heuristic Evaluation

An agreed-upon set of usability best practices used to evaluate an interface

- This is a usability inspection method that asks evaluators to assess an interface against a set of agreed-upon best practices or usability "rules of thumb."

- Unlike usability tests with actual users, these evaluations enlist team members to inspect and fix baseline usability problems before user testing.

- When heuristics are applied repeatedly during an iterative design process, the principles will become more intuitive and usability problems easier to detect.

- Novices trained on heuristics and evaluators familiar with the subject and usability practices conduct evaluations.

- The method can help detect critical but missing dialogue elements early in the design process, as well as heuristics that are working well.

- When used in the middle phases of the design process, even with low-fidelity prototypes, evaluations can make later usability tests more effective.

See also Cognitive Walkthrough • Evaluative Research • Prototyping

Aesthetic and
minimalist design

Flexibility and
efficiency of use

Error prevention

A sample of Molich and Nielsen's original ten heuristics, adapted
and applied to iPhone apps.

047

Image Boards

A collage of pictures, illustrations, or brand imagery to visually communicate aspects of design intent

- They are used to visually convey an essential description of design aesthetics, style, audience, or context.

- Images convey the particular styles, colors, products, brands, and environments associated with the designer's interpretation of a given aesthetic.

- A user-based image board portrays a target audience, conveyed through their clothing, preferred brands, environments, transportation, and social interests.

- An environment-based image board visually shows sample interiors, furniture, lighting, fixtures, and conveys color palettes and atmospheric tone.

- The creation of image boards can serve internally as a consensus artifact for design teams, representing an agreed-upon version of a design aesthetic or context.

- Externally, image boards are powerful tools for communicating design intent to clients, clarifying an aesthetic direction or targeted audience.

See also   Mind Mapping • Stakeholder Maps • Territory Maps

Image boards helped a design team understand the culture and spirit of teenage girls, informing the visual and verbal language for a role-playing game.

048

Interviews

Conversation to collect first-hand accounts of
experience, opinions, attitudes, and perceptions

- They are best conducted in person to include nuances
  of personal expression and body language, but may
  also be conducted by phone or social media.

- They may follow a script of questions or simply have a
  guiding topic, which allows for flexible detours in
  conversational form.

- Stakeholder interviews focus on information from
  specific roles or people who may have a vested
  interest in the particular inquiry.

- Key informant interviews concentrate on people who
  have specialized or expert knowledge to contribute.

- Interviews of couples or groups should be moderated
  so conversations are not dominated by one person.

- Interviews can be more productive when based
  around artifacts, the inspiration behind methods,
  personal inventories, and picture cards.

See also   Contextual Inquiry • Questionnaires • Surveys

Interviews are a common research method, often used to verify and humanize data collected using complementary methods such as questionnaires and observations.

049

KJ Technique

A silent sort method to help teams work through a problem space and prioritize focus

- The KJ Technique is a consensus-building exercise that helps teams externalize a complicated range of ideas and information.

- It focuses the team on one question and sets everyone to work on the same task at the same time.

- Everyone in the group writes as many problems, data, insights, or opinions as they can think of, in silence.

- Sticky notes are posted simultaneously, opening up the opportunity for a holistic assessment of the problem space rather than competing opinions.

- By providing a framework where everyone silently works together, decisions are made democratically, with little or no opportunities for coercion.

- Working efficiently, a team can organize their notes into an affinity diagram.

See also Affinity Diagramming • Value Opportunity Analysis • Weighted Matrix

Everyone writes all of their concerns...

...then, notes are sorted in silence...

Using the KJ Technique, team members independently identify their respective concerns and project requirements on sticky notes and then silently cluster similar concerns and challenges.

050

Kano Analysis

Helps determine and prioritize which product attributes are most important to the customer

- By assigning each product attribute to one of five categories, customer values regarding satisfaction can be revealed.

- **Required** (*atari mae* or "quality element") are the baseline features that must be included, such as privacy, safety, and security.

- **Desired** (*ichi gen teki* or "one-dimensional quality element") are attributes that when included, increase the perceived value of the product.

- **Exciter/Delighter** (*mi ryoku teki* or "attractive quality element") are a source of surprise based on latent customer needs, improving measures of satisfaction.

- **Neutral** (*mu kan shin* or "indifferent quality element") represent features that customers don't have strong feelings for either way.

- **Anti-feature** (*gyaku* or "reverse quality element") attributes provide insight into what you should leave out of a product.

See also Desirability Testing • Surveys • Value Opportunity Analysis

The Kano Analysis can help you make informed decisions about which product features to improve first or in what order to add features.

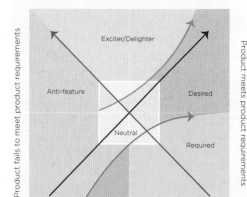

Question 1: If product attribute is present, the customer feels...

		Satisfied	Neutral	Dissatisfied
Question 2: If product attribute is absent, the customer feels...	Satisfied	Questionable	Anti-feature	Anti-feature
	Neutral	Exciter/ Delighter	Neutral	Anti-feature
	Dissatisfied	Desired	Required	Questionable

051

Key Performance Indicators (KPIs)

Measurements of how well you are doing against quantifiable, widely accepted business goals

- KPIs measure where you were yesterday and where you are today, in relationship to where you are trying to go in terms of some predefined business objective.

- Each KPI is a measurement derived from an individual's interaction with your product or service.

- KPIs are great for quantifying behavior or value metrics (e.g., the ratio of people who abandon their shopping cart versus those who complete the sale).

- As an action-oriented measure, KPIs can help:

  – Recognize, prioritize, and react as issues occur

  – Meaningfully summarize and compare data and use it to your advantage

  – Document a business case for change

  – Foster an ongoing organizational understanding of how people respond to your product or service

- The KPI reporting process needs to be ongoing and frequent enough so that fluctuations can be immediately course-corrected.

See also   Site Search Analytics • Web Analytics

	Senior Strategists	Tactical Team Members
Content Sites	• Average page views per visit • Average cost per visit • Average revenue per visit • % high, med, low frequency visitors	• % of visitors using search • % high, med, low click depth visits • Landing page bounce rate • RSS/email subscription conversion rate
Marketing Sites	• Lead generation conversion rate • Average cost per lead generated • Average (estimated) revenue per visit • Average cost per lead generated	• Landing page bounce rate • Average searches per visit • % zero yield searches • Lead generation rate for campaigns
Customer Service Sites	• Average time to respond to email inquiries • % high, low customer satisfaction • % new and returning customers	• % high, medium, low click depth visits • % zero yield searches • Form completion rates • Download completion rates
Online Retailers	• Order conversion rate • Buyer conversion rate • Average revenue per visit • Average cost per conversion • % high, low satisfaction customers	• Search to purchase conversion rate • % of low recency visitors • Cart and checkout completion rate • Order conversion rate by campaign type • Zero yield searches

This shows the recommended KPIs for four popular business models and which internal team should monitor them.

052

Laddering

An interviewing technique that reveals connections between a product's characteristics and personal values

- It builds on Means–End Theory, which posits that people make purchasing decisions based on consequences afforded by using the product.

- Connects a product's obvious physical characteristics to values by repeatedly asking "Why" questions.

- As the conversation builds on itself to reveal what a person values, the "ladder" is constructed that connects product attributes to the consequences and to the individual's values.

- Consequences are the benefit or the impact that the product has on a person and reveal another layer about what is important.

- Values expose the root cause behind why a product resonates profoundly with a person.

- Seven values are often the motivation behind purchasing behavior: self-esteem, accomplishment, belonging, self-fulfillment, family, satisfaction, and security.

See also   Interviews • Triading • Value Opportunity Analysis

Laddering is used to reveal the connection between a product's obvious physical characteristics and the deeper personal values that it reinforces in a customer's life.

053

Literature Reviews

The written collection and synthesis of research on a given topic

- These are intended to distill information from published sources, capturing the essence of previous research or projects to inform the current project.

- Strategies for organizing may be categorical, chrono-logical, thematic, or methodological.

- Internet resources have expedited searches but judgment is needed to ensure relevance and credibility of sources.

- May include books, chapters, journal and magazine articles, theses and dissertations, corporate and academic websites and blogs, and past design projects.

- The guiding factor in selecting literature should be relevance, clearly suggesting how it informed the design investigation.

- Literature reviews should be accurately referenced using a consistent bibliographic style.

See also   Evidence-Based Design • Secondary Research • Unobtrusive Measures

Extracting salient information from precedent research
and projects through comprehensive literature reviews is
a critical step in laying the foundation and contextualizing
the design inquiry.

054

The Love Letter & The Breakup Letter

Writing to express sentiments to a personified product or service

- The Love Letter conveys what people feel during moments of connection with a product, including delight, infatuation, and loyalty.

- The Breakup Letter provides insight about how, when, and where a relationship with a product turned sour, to understand why people abandon a product.

- Both exercises are great techniques to use in a group dynamic, including design workshops, group interviews, and icebreaker sessions.

- Ask participants to spend no more than ten minutes on a letter and then volunteers can read theirs aloud.

- The physical letters are important research artifacts, while video can capture participant expressions and voices.

- Methods like the Love Letter and the Breakup Letter build our empathic knowledge base of how people experience and personify designs.

See also   Design Workshops • Desirability Testing • Value Opportunity Analysis

The Love Letter and Breakup Letter allow participants to express their love or disappointment to a product or service with a handwritten letter.

Method courtesy of Smart Design

055

Mental Model Diagrams

A framework aligning task behaviors, beliefs, and emotions with product and service features

- Can help you articulate root causes behind behaviors and develop solutions that deeply resonate with people.

- Diverse groups identified for study are called task-based audience segments, each usually comprised of at least four people.

- Diagrams are built from the bottom up, using singularly focused behaviors, beliefs, and emotions derived from interviews or diary studies.

- The top half of the diagram represents the behaviors, beliefs, and emotions people have as they set out to accomplish a task.

- The bottom half of the diagram represents the features, product, and service offering.

- The goal is to help teams make appropriate product development strategies that align with how people already approach problem solving in their daily lives.

See also   Diary Studies • Interviews • Task Analysis

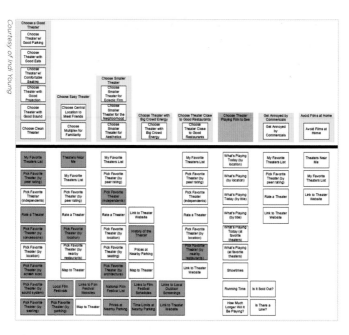

The top half of the diagram represents behaviors, beliefs, or emotions. The bottom half represents the features, services, or products available in your current offering.

056

Mind Mapping

A visual thinking tool to organize and understand the complexities of a problem space

- It can help generate ideas and develop concepts using the following steps:

  1. Identify a themed focus question to draw in the center.

  2. Label extensions with simple verb-noun pairs or noun clusters.

  3. Connect primary and secondary connections with lines to create meaning.

  4. Continue free associations until all relevant information is represented.

  5. Before declaring the map complete, reflect for a while.

- The map provides a nonlinear means of externalizing the information in our heads so that we can interpret, consolidate, communicate, store, and retrieve it.

- The map allows us to summarize and test assumptions, make and break connections, and consider alternatives while we shape data into themes and patterns.

See also   Brainstorm Graphic Organizers • Collage • Concept Mapping

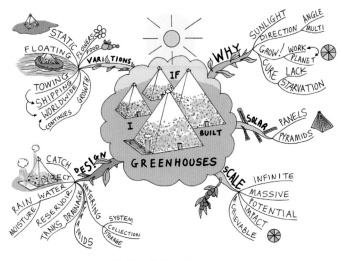

© Paul Foreman http://www.mindmapinspiration.com

Mind mapping allows us to simultaneously identify the subject of the map, relationships between the components, and understand the relative importance of the information represented.

057

Observation

Attentive looking and systematic recording of people, artifacts, environments, events, behaviors, and interactions

- Semi-structured observation typically describes ethnographic methods in the exploratory phase of design.

- Ethnographic observations should be flexible, yet systematic, careful, and well documented with notes, sketches, photographs, or video.

- Semi-structured observations are typically synthesized for guiding design inspiration, but content analysis may be performed to uncover themes or patterns.

- Structured, or systematic observation, is formalized by pre-structure utilizing worksheets to track time intervals, behavioral categories, or counted successes and errors.

- If sample sizes are large enough, results can be quantified for analysis otherwise, it is common to look for patterns or trends across observations.

- Observations should differentiate between factual behaviors witnessed and inferences, speculating the meaning and motivations behind actions.

See also   AEIOU • Fly-on-the-Wall Observation • Participant Observation

Documented contextual observations from a customer-centered study of the library experience to inform redesign.

058

Parallel Prototyping

Simultaneously exploring multiple design ideas
before selecting one approach

- This can help teams from fixating on a design direction
  too early, improve the nature of design critiques, and
  lead to more effective design results.

- Designers quickly and independently create a
  divergent range of low-fidelity prototypes and then
  submit designs to testing by end users or to heuristic
  evaluation by experts.

- Evaluations help designers to thoughtfully consider
  how people react to individual elements of the design
  and which accomplish the project's intended goals.

- The method shifts focus from the designer onto the
  design, promoting a safe environment where critiques
  are more engaging, less personal, and less stressful.

- The method promotes team collaboration and builds
  rapport, as designers will often merge and refine
  others' concepts into their subsequent designs.

See also Design Charette • Prototyping •
Research Through Design

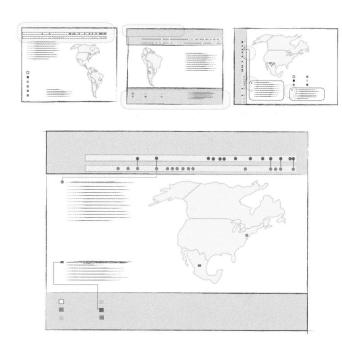

By simultaneously designing and testing multiple approaches, there is a better chance that the final design will represent the best qualities of all design options.

059

Participant Observation

Immersive membership in an activity, context, culture, or subculture

- A participant observation (PO) researcher forms deep connections and empathy by experiencing events in the same way as the people they are studying.

- PO is a foundational method of anthropology, adapted for design use through time-limited engagements.

- Systematic observation and recording are critical to document physical aspects of the environment, behaviors, interactions, language, motivations, and perceptions of the participants.

- Marginal participants blend into an environment as natural observers of an activity or event.

- Full participants take on a membership role or may already occupy a role that allows for full participation.

- Participant observers need to stay vigilant to retain some measure of objectivity and to avoid undue influence on member behaviors.

See also   Design Ethnography • Fly-on-the-Wall Observation • Observation

Marginal participant observation of transit riders for a service design project on "commutenity," promoting community and reinforcing positive behaviors among bus riders.

060

Participatory Action Research (PAR)

A cyclical, collaborative process that seeks to intentionally change members of the inquiry

- The mission is to change the community, or policies under study, differentiated from objective methods that seek only to describe, understand, and explain.

- With an overtone of empowerment, emancipation, and activism, the approach has been popular in education, feminist research, and social justice.

- The process is dynamic and cyclical in its sequence of planning, taking action, observing, evaluating, and critical reflection.

- Specific research methods tend to be flexible, qualitative, and ethnographic, including traditional observations, participant observation, and interviews.

- New movements in social design suggest a natural affiliation with participatory methods, including collaborative design workshops and creative tool kits.

- It is a powerful process when aligned with issues identified by a community, inspiring action to be applied directly to problems.

See also   Case Studies • Participatory Design

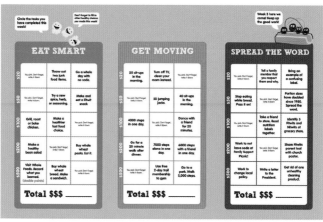

In research designing a health literacy game, participants described undergoing improved self-image, better physical and psychological well-being, and positive reinforcement from friends and family.

061

Participatory Design

A human-centered approach advocating codesign engagement with users and stakeholders

- Participatory design has its roots in Scandinavia in the 1970s, where computer professionals worked with unions to integrate new technology into the workplace.

- Participatory design encompasses several methods, unified by face-to-face contact in activity-based codesign engagements.

- Methods include cultural probes, diary studies, photo studies, collage, flexible modeling, role-playing, creative tool kits, and design workshops.

- Participatory design respects the creative insight of participants to inspire and help guide the design process and to respond to design outcomes.

- A framework of participatory design describes the form of method or technique (making, telling, and enacting) and purpose.

- Purposes are probing participants for self-discovery, priming for further participation, understanding current experience, and generation of future scenarios and concepts.

See also   Creative Toolkits • Design Workshops

In this participatory design project on appliance design for the aging population, participants use creative toolkits for design input and offer feedback on prototypes.

062

Personal Inventories

Representative collections of artifacts selected by the participant for the designer-researcher

- This allows the designer to see and understand the relevance of objects in a user's life in order to inspire design themes and insight.

- It is most commonly solicited through paired methods such as guided tours, contextual interviews, and photo and diary studies.

- As a component of touchstone tours, participants talk about the things they own as they walk the researcher through their home or other environment.

- As an element of photo studies, participants document the objects of meaning, often with companion notations.

- Interviews probe for object meaning, the role in a participant's life, acquisition, use, placement, and how they might feel if the object were lost or damaged.

- Personal inventories may focus on certain types of objects, but are more commonly driven by the participant, who identifies items of significance.

See also   Artifact Analysis • Diary Studies • Touchstone Tours

Personal inventories can reveal the significance of objects, but may rely on the designer to extract insight about the user and context for design inquiry.

063

Personas

Representative human profiles based on archetypal descriptions of users from research

- Crafted from information collected from real users through sound field research and captures common behaviors in meaningful and relatable profiles.

- They are useful in humanizing design focus, testing scenarios, and aiding in design communication.

- Human descriptions facilitate easy empathy and communication, while distinctions create useful targets for responsible design.

- Affinity diagramming or other methods can be used to cluster similarities across users to form archetypes.

- Personas are typically page-length descriptions, with a name, a photo, and a story describing key aspects of life, goals, and behaviors.

- Personas are used as a lasting human reference by teams throughout all phases of the project.

- Provide a persuasive human reference when communicating research summaries and scenarios to clients.

See also Scenario Description Swimlanes • Scenarios • User Journey Maps

This is a persona of a college student. The majority of information about the persona is visually illustrated to reflect her knowledge, activities and interests, influencers, and backstory.

064

Photo Studies

Self-documentation of a participant's life and interactions

- Common in exploratory research as a method for understanding the world of users, particularly when engaging in territory unfamiliar to the designer.

- To initiate a photo study, participants are provided with a camera or instructed how their own cameras are to be used for the purposes of the research.

- Participants are given general instructions on what to document, or they may be instructed to take images at certain times or when feeling a particular way.

- Photo studies are most often used as a complement to other methods: for example, diary studies or the experience sampling method.

- The designer may rely solely on the photographs and participant notes for synthesis or have the participant explain or sort their photos.

- Patterns and themes might emerge within several photos from multiple participants.

See also   Cultural Probes • Diary Studies • Experience Sampling Method

Collected photos from a crowdsourced photo study on energy use reveal a diverse range of interpretations on the subject matter for design consideration.

065

Picture Cards

Cards with images and words help people think about and share true experiences

- In a session, participants recall an experience, using the cards to support memories and evoke conversation.

- Picture cards stem from activity theory, which asserts, "the human mind is the product of our interaction with people and artifacts in the context of everyday activity."

- Cards are created with images and caption text relevant to the research inquiry, but connected to the personal accounts of participant lives.

- Card sets should account for current and future product and service experiences and include blank cards for details that might emerge during sessions.

- The method should be used flexibly, adding, subtracting, and editing picture cards in pretesting prior to field use and even between research sessions.

- The cards can be used for sorting current products and services used and "sketching" future scenarios, which are laid out as a story unfolds.

See also   Directed Storytelling • Interviews • Touchstone Tours

In a picture card session, cards are sorted by participants and used to guide storytelling of past experiences and the sketching of future scenarios.

066

Prototyping

The tangible creation of artifacts, at various levels of resolution, for development and testing of ideas

- Prototypes are essential for early and iterative concept testing by the design team, clients, and potential users.

- Low-fidelity prototyping is common throughout early ideation processes in all design disciplines, appearing as concept sketches, storyboards, or sketch models.

- A common method of low-fidelity prototyping in interface and software design is paper prototyping, with printed pages representing interface screens.

- In graphic design, the "comp" serves as a low-fidelity prototype, presenting a mocked-up version of a proposed printed piece, usually for client review.

- In industrial design, low-fidelity prototypes may be sketch models intended for iterative design review or as proof of concept models to test form and scale.

- High-fidelity prototypes represent the appearance of the final product in look and feel and basic functionality, through interactive computer or physical models.

See also   Experience Prototyping • Research Through Design • Storyboards

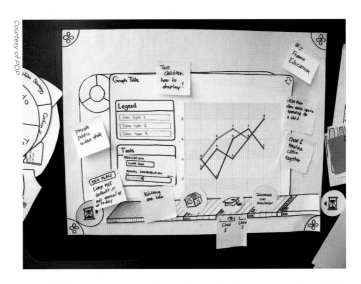

Low-fidelity prototypes of interface behaviors are used to build consensus and understanding among project team members and clients.

067

Questionnaires

Self-reported information about thoughts, feelings, perceptions, behaviors, or attitudes

- One of the primary tools used to collect survey information, the other being interviews.

- They are simple to produce and administer, but careful attention should be paid to question wording and response options, sequencing, and length.

- Factors in securing a good response rate in both print and digital questionnaires include appearance, clarity, instructions, arrangement, design, and layout.

- Open-ended questions provide opportunity for depth of response, whereas closed-ended questions are easier to numerically analyze and communicate.

- To maintain question neutrality while also gaining an indication of strength of response, Likert scale questions are highly recommended.

- They are commonly triangulated with other methods, such as observation, to supplement the data with personal insights and verify self-reported behaviors.

See also   Interviews • Semantic Differential • Surveys

Questionnaires can be used as a component of various forms of research: for example, as part of a diary study or an element of product evaluation.

068

Rapid Iterative Testing & Evaluation (RITE)

A powerful formative usability inspection method that identifies early interface problems

- This is rigorous method used to evaluate and identify interface problems, quickly fix them, and then empirically verify the efficacy of the fixes.

- RITE explores user behavior insights relative to design direction as opposed to summative goals, which measure usability issues.

- Prototypes are changed as soon as problems are identified and the team agrees to a solution, and the fix is then retested with more participants.

- Scheduled tests continue after each design change until there is a string of successes with no failures.

- Domain knowledge can help observers prioritize fixes based on their judgment of true problems versus what is an artifact of a particular participant.

- RITE begins when you have a low-fidelity prototype to test, in order to fix issues before time and resources are spent producing a high-fidelity prototype.

See also   Prototyping • Think-Aloud Protocol • Usability Testing

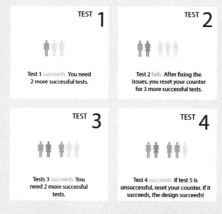

TEST **1**

Test 1 succeeds. You need 2 more successful tests.

TEST **2**

Test 2 fails. After fixing the issues, you reset your counter for 3 more successful tests.

TEST **3**

Tests 3 succeeds. You need 2 more successful tests.

TEST **4**

Test 4 succeeds. If test 5 is unsuccessful, reset your counter. If it succeeds, the design succeeds!

Totals: 5 participants
       2 revised prototypes

An example test cycle using the RITE Method.

069

Remote Moderated Research

Remotely observing users completing tasks on their own devices in context

- A participant completes tasks while thinking out loud while software allows a remote researcher and observers to review behaviors and ask questions.

- Remote Moderated Research can reveal deep insights into contexts of use that cannot be replicated in a controlled lab environment.

- The method exposes rich, qualitative data about a participant's native computer and possibly his or her physical environment.

- With "live recruiting," participants can be intercepted when they begin a process, and research can be initiated immediately upon their consent.

- Live recruiting allows the research team to observe behavior in a task that the participant has selected as important and relevant as opposed to one assigned.

See also Stakeholder Walkthrough • Time-Aware Research • Usability Testing

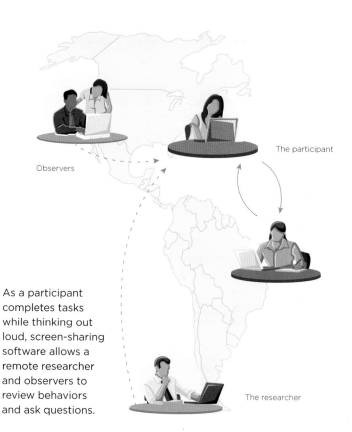

Observers

The participant

As a participant completes tasks while thinking out loud, screen-sharing software allows a remote researcher and observers to review behaviors and ask questions.

The researcher

070

Research Through Design

Utilizing the design process as a reflective research activity to enhance design practices

- This examines the tools and processes of design thinking and making within the design project, bridging theory and building knowledge.

- It is constituted by the design process itself, including the critical act of recording and communicating the steps, experiments, and iterations of design.

- Designers utilize their work, including sketches, drawings, models, and prototypes to interrogate ideas, test hypotheses, and pose new questions.

- As an approach to interaction design, this method integrates models and theories with technical knowledge in the design process.

- Designers who conduct their research through creative, critically reflective practice may at once be responding to a design brief and a set of larger questions.

- Documentation is critical to contextualize and communicate design action, advance scholarship, and enhance the inventory of design resources.

See also   Case Studies • Evidence-Based Design • Prototyping

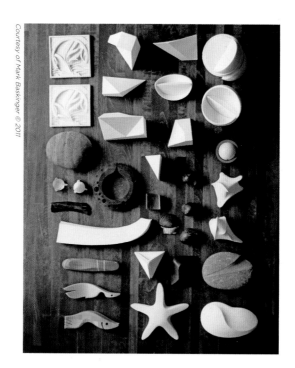

These form studies embody an inquiry into materials, surfaces, volumes, and edges, informing research and teaching in the experimentation and generation of form.

071

Role-Playing

Acting the role of the user in realistic scenarios to present empathic design opportunities

- Role-playing is usually guided by describing a general situation or suggestions for actions to be performed, tasks to be accomplished, or goals to be reached.

- Members of the design team have to be willing to play and improvise, yet be cautious to avoid exchanges that can lead to hurtful or upsetting words or actions.

- Debriefing after role-playing is critical to make sense of what occurred and to assess genuine feelings that may have resulted from the session.

- Role-playing is difficult to document by the actors involved, so it is useful to have other team members record the sessions using photos and notes or video.

- Role-playing is useful when direct observation is not feasible or ethical: for example, for personally sensitive situations or where access to the users is restricted.

See also   Bodystorming • Experience Prototyping • Simulation Exercises

Members of design teams engaged in role-playing have to be willing and realistic participants. Here, designers are enthusiastically role-playing services for parents with young children.

072

Scenario Description Swimlanes

A holistic visualization of the activities of multiple actors in a flow of events

- It can benefit any project where several processes or actors have to come together to shape the outcome of the same flow of events.

- Multiple scenario description swimlanes should be created from user research, each focused on its own specific story with the following elements:

  - **Storyboard lane:** Captures the events in a user story using comics, photographs, illustrations, or sketches.

  - **User Experience lane:** This is a flowchart depicting the story with more detail and insight into the process of the user experience.

  - **Business Process lane:** This is the business logic providing the required processes that facilitates the steps of the user experience.

  - **Tools and Systems lane:** Back-end technology that is involved to support user actions and business goals.

- The method visually connects an overarching user story with problems being solved at both a macro perspective and detailed micro view.

See also Personas • Scenarios • Stakeholder Maps

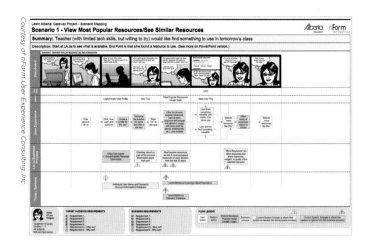

The visual nature of swimlanes provides a bird's-eye view of the moving parts within a story, helping to get everyone on the same page.

073

Scenarios

A narrative exploring the future use of a product from a user's point of view

- A scenario is a believable narrative, usually set in the future, of a person's experience as he or she engages with a product or a service.

- By making design ideas explicit and concrete, the design team can empathetically envision the future ways in which a product is likely to be used.

- The scenario should focus efforts on building culturally meaningful artifacts that augment actual human activity, rather than designing toward technical requirements.

- Scenarios bring personas to life. Both deliverables therefore reinforce the value of the other.

- Scenarios should range from baseline, status quo to high-stress situations with less-than-optimal conditions.

- Scenarios can be written to follow a traditional story arc, with a trigger event, scene, and preconditions, and task resolution with technology that assists and delights.

See also   Business Origami • Personas • Speed Dating

A goal-oriented scenario with a customer persona, showing key interactions and barriers to a successful library experience.

074

Secondary Research

Information collected and synthesized from existing data and sources

- Secondary research establishes what has been done and what hasn't, identifying opportunity gaps to help suggest a research direction and methods.

- It is sometimes referred to as desk research, in contrast to primary research conducted as fieldwork or empirical research.

- Sources may include books, research papers, journal articles, and conference papers, records and statistics, or any number of other archives.

- In design, research might include precedent projects, products or documented case studies, photographs, maps, diagrams, and other visual support records.

- It is traditionally summarized in systematic reviews or literature reviews, with full citations of sources.

- In design, secondary research can also be collected into visual summaries or blogs, for shared viewing, sorting, synthesis, and the crafting of narratives.

See also   Case Studies • Literature Reviews • Unobtrusive Measures

The WorldCat database allows users to search the collections and services of more than 10,000 libraries worldwide, including the option to select specific media types.

075

Semantic Differential

A linguistic tool designed to measure people's attitudes toward a topic, event, object, or activity

- The semantic differential asks respondents to indicate where on a continuum of antonyms a concept is best described (e.g., pleasant—unpleasant).

- The three dimensions to classify concepts are evaluation (e.g., valuable–worthless), potency (e.g., strong–weak), and activity (e.g., active–passive).

- Concepts should be chosen based on research objectives and should be meaningful to respondents.

- Poles should be randomized so that negative and positive connotations don't always fall on the same side.

- A seven-point scale is preferred because it provides a neutral midpoint, which could indicate apathy, indecisiveness, or social relevance.

- How various concepts are mapped in a semantic space reflect their differences in connotative meaning.

See also   Laddering • Questionnaires • Surveys

Please rate this human on the adjective scales below.

		1	2	3	4	5	6	7
1=Awful	7=Nice	○	○	○	○	○	○	○
1=Machinelike	7=Humanlike	○	○	○	○	○	○	○
1=Artificial	7=Lifelike	○	○	○	○	○	○	○
1=Unpleasant	7=Pleasant	○	○	○	○	○	○	○
1=Fake	7=Natural	○	○	○	○	○	○	○
1=Unfriendly	7=Friendly	○	○	○	○	○	○	○
1=Unconscious	7=Conscious	○	○	○	○	○	○	○
1=Unkind	7=Kind	○	○	○	○	○	○	○

Please rate this human on the adjective scales below.

		1	2	3	4	5	6	7
1=Awful	7=Nice	○	○	○	○	○	○	○
1=Machinelike	7=Humanlike	○	○	○	○	○	○	○
1=Artificial	7=Lifelike	○	○	○	○	○	○	○
1=Unpleasant	7=Pleasant	○	○	○	○	○	○	○
1=Fake	7=Natural	○	○	○	○	○	○	○
1=Unfriendly	7=Friendly	○	○	○	○	○	○	○
1=Unconscious	7=Conscious	○	○	○	○	○	○	○
1=Unkind	7=Kind	○	○	○	○	○	○	○

Eight semantic differential scales were used to investigate the degree to which a person's cultural background influences one's perception of a robot's anthropomorphism and likeability.

076

Shadowing

An observational method tracking someone closely through his or her daily routines

- Provides key insight into a participant's activities and decision patterns, collecting insights through the detailed nuance of firsthand, real-time exposure.

- Observations should be well documented, with photographs, detailed notes and sketches, or audio.

- Ideally, several team members will complete shadowing exercises across representative users, to begin crafting a general picture of patterns.

- Cooperation is necessary and a respectful distance should be maintained to avoid interruption to natural routines or behavior change as a result of being observed.

- Typically, interactions with the person being shadowed are kept to a minimum, asking pertinent questions about behaviors after the shadowing session.

- Subtle covert shadowing may be utilized to observe public behaviors: for example, following students on campus to determine common pathways.

See also Behavioral Mapping • Fly-on-the-Wall Observation • Touchstone Tours

In a study of the relationship between food providers and consumers in creating sustainable food communities, grocery shoppers were shadowed, asked about their decisions, and photographed.

077

Simulation Exercises

Deep approximations of human or environmental conditions

- Effective simulations forge a tangible, immersive sense of real-life user experience to influence design sensitivity and decisions.

- Simulated real-world conditions can provide empathic emotional experiences or test functional interactions like response time and decision-making.

- These exercises have been used in military, aircraft and NASA training, driving simulators, and virtual worlds.

- In design, exercises might approximate the limitations experienced by people with physical disabilities, brain injuries, or age-related sense and cognition deficits.

- Low-tech simulations can utilize wheelchairs, manipulated glasses lenses, or blindfolds to empathically experience restricted mobility or visual impairment.

- Designers are involved in the creation of simulated environments such as video games, virtual or augmented reality, physical spaces, and artifacts.

See also Bodystorming • Experience Prototyping • Role-Playing

Researchers perform tasks wearing the "Age Gain Now Empathy System" (AGNES), developed in the MIT AgeLab to simulate the dexterity, mobility, strength, and balance of a 74-year-old.

078

Site Search Analytics

Reporting and analyzing user queries submitted as search criteria on a site

- Analyzing words and phrases entered into a search provides insight into what people are looking for in order to evaluate how well content meets those needs.

- Site Search Analytics can bolster customer retention, satisfaction, and conversion rates, aligning user-centered activity to measurable business goals.

- For qualitative research, understanding user intent and the information people want from your site can help you evaluate and improve the quality of the search results.

- For quantitative data, a Zipf distribution represents the statistical majority of search terms within a given time frame, pinpointing which should be optimized.

- If you are in launch & monitor phase, relate site search performance metrics to your organization's existing Key Performance Indicators (KPIs).

- The data revealed by Site Search Analytics can help you monitor and improve your application's overall performance.

See also   Content Inventory & Audit •
Key Performance Indicators • Web Analytics

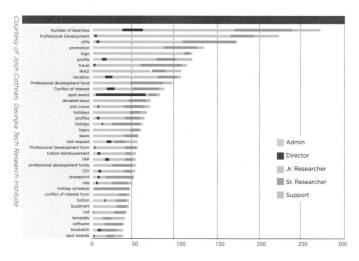

Here is an example of a typical Site Search Analytics Zipf distribution, where a small number of search terms represent the most popular searches.

079

Speed Dating

The rapid review of multiple design concepts by multiple users in quick succession

- Exposes people to design ideas via storyboards and simulated environments before expensive technical prototypes are built, using the following process:

  - Conduct contextual field research via methods such as interviews, role-playing, artifact analysis, directed storytelling, diary studies, and cultural probes.

  - Create storyboards to elicit an emotional, empathic reaction to relatable characters in convincing scenarios, based on the needs uncovered by research.

  - Speed date storyboards to a group of people followed by focus questions to help design teams understand what is in the users' minds.

  - Articulate misunderstandings, refine scenarios, and consider new design opportunities based on user rankings of needs and effectiveness.

  - Construct a simulated environment to allow people to act out a role from the revised scenarios, observing how users deal with specific problems in context.

See also   Experience Prototyping • Scenarios • Storyboards

ENACTMENT ONE:
THE PARENT BUTTON

What kinds of and how much virtual information can be comfortable displayed for parents to see?

ENACTMENT TWO:
MULTIPLE SELF-PRESENTATIONS

How would your different online personas look if they were all visible in one place?

Speed dating allows for structured engagements across multiple scenarios, creating new understanding about potential design opportunities to consider and problem areas that should be avoided.

080

Stakeholder Maps

A visual representation of key constituents of a design project

- Stakeholder maps provide a visual reference point for the design team, setting the stage for user-centered research and design development.

- Include people who will benefit from the project, those who hold power, those who may be adversely affected, and even those who may sabotage designed outcomes.

- Stakeholders can be identified by general roles (e.g., nurses), specific roles (e.g., chief of surgery), or by actual people (e.g., Linda, resident physician).

- From an initial sketch or list using whiteboards, cards, or paper, the map evolves into a structure with hierarchy and key relationships between roles or people.

- Stakeholder maps can take on a variety of forms, with a mix of text, photos, and graphics and use of scale, line, and proximity to express relationships.

See also   Stakeholder Walkthrough • Territory Maps

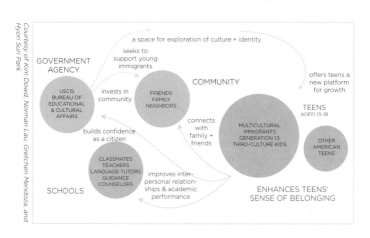

a space for exploration of culture + identity

seeks to support young immigrants

GOVERNMENT AGENCY

offers teens a new platform for growth

USCIS BUREAU OF EDUCATIONAL & CULTURAL AFFAIRS

invests in community

FRIENDS FAMILY NEIGHBORS

COMMUNITY

TEENS AGED 13-18

builds confidence as a citizen

connects with family + friends

MULTICULTURAL IMMIGRANTS GENERATION 1.5 THIRD-CULTURE KIDS

OTHER AMERICAN TEENS

CLASSMATES TEACHERS LANGUAGE TUTORS GUIDANCE COUNSELORS

improves inter-personal relation-ships & academic performance

SCHOOLS

ENHANCES TEENS' SENSE OF BELONGING

This is a stakeholder map consolidating key players and roles for the design of a social networking application for teenage immigrants during cultural transition to the United States.

081

Stakeholder Walkthrough

Early prototype evaluations by a team of end users, stakeholders, and designers

- This brings multiple stakeholders together to step through and evaluate a task-based scenario from the end user's perspective.

- As a group usability inspection method, it requires a diverse range of skills and perspectives to identify and consider problems early in the prototyping process.

- Attendees should be told that they will be asked to take the end user's perspective as opposed to defending a system or design/development view.

- The whole team works together, focusing on usability problem detection and brainstorming solutions.

- Team walkthroughs can be more costly than individual techniques, but they have proven to be more effective.

- Recurring attendance in stakeholder walkthroughs will sharpen the team's empathic response to their end user's frustrations, challenges, and perspectives.

See also   Design Charette • Stakeholder Maps • Usability Testing

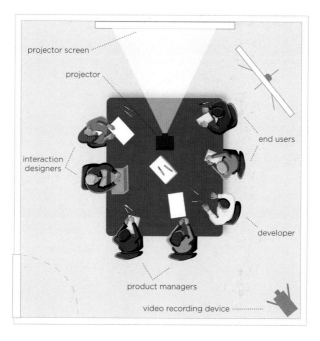

projector screen

projector

interaction designers

end users

developer

product managers

video recording device

Scheduling stakeholder walkthroughs early in the design process combines perspectives of representative end users, stakeholders, developers, and members of the design and research team.

082

Storyboards

A visual narrative that generates empathy and communicates the context for proposed design solutions

• Five design practices common to visual storytelling:

1. Refine drawings so that they show enough context, but not so much that details begin to distract from the purpose of the storyboard.

2. Use text to supplement the visuals in a storyboard when it would otherwise take too much effort to illustrate a concept or idea.

3. Emphasize people, products, or both, depending on whether you want to elicit an emotional impact or get technical or evaluative feedback on the concept.

4. Use three to six panels to communicate an idea, with each storyboard focused on one salient concept.

5. To show time lapses, use design elements such as clocks, calendars, or the movement of the sun.

See also Personas • Role-Playing • Speed Dating

Do you ever wish you had someone of a similar culture/background to talk with about type 2 diabetes?

Person is diagnosed with type 2 diabetes. Doctor leaves, and nurse comes in to set up the person with a mentor.

He or she inputs criteria for a mentor, and system finds a match with another person with type 2 diabetes.

The mentor answers questions as the person learns how to manage his or her diabetes.

Do you ever wish you had someone to help your spouse/family to understand what you are dealing with and how best to support you?

Family doesn't know how they can help their loved one with their type 2 diabetes.

Trained caregiver answers the family's questions and provides helpful tips to be supportive.

Family is active in providing care for their loved one.

Storyboards shape social, environmental, and temporal factors into a compelling narrative and help design teams to carefully consider how products and services could improve lives.

083

Surveys

Collection of self-reported information about thoughts, feelings, perceptions, behaviors, or attitudes

- This is an efficient tool for collecting a lot of versatile data in a short time frame, with results that can be analyzed statistically.

- Survey questionnaires can be either self-completed or read to participants and completed by the researcher.

- Interviews can be conducted in person, by phone, or through various communication technologies.

- Like any self-reporting, surveys may not accurately reflect true thoughts, feelings, perceptions, or behaviors.

- Surveys should therefore be carefully designed and administered and paired with complementary methods such as observations or contextual inquiry.

- There are various types of questions: closed/open, general/specific, factual, hypothetical, judgmental, and comparative.

- Questions should avoid leading to an answer or blaming the participant as wrong or at fault.

See also Interviews • Questionnaires

The "Produce Proposal Wall" used a survey method allowing customers to communicate what they want in the grocery store, while fostering dialogue and building community.

084

Task Analysis

Workflow analysis, including user actions, system response, and environmental context

- Task encompasses any physical actions and mental processes as activities used to achieve goals and any information flows within the system environment.

- Designers typically incorporate a blend of qualitative and quantitative approaches to gain insight into user and task processes.

- The method targets user options, tools, decision points, common mistakes, corrections, inputs/outputs, frequency and importance of tasks, and risks of failure.

- Actions in task decomposition can be organized by categories, such as purpose, cues, objects, method, and options.

- A Hierarchical Task Analysis (HTA) typically results in tree diagrams or flowcharts, which can be verified by walk-through tests.

- Task analysis is useful for all design disciplines, ranging from navigation of software to wayfinding in the built environment.

See also   Contextual Inquiry • Ergonomic Analysis • Observation

A task analysis grid visualizes stakeholder scenarios and prioritized tasks. Each column describes a scenario, a task, and the subtasks necessary to complete the task.

085

Territory Maps

A visual representation of shared content focus to set research and design activities

- The creation process draws on the preconceptions and knowledge of design team members, contributed in a shared vision.

- The simplicity of the diagram is deceptively powerful, representing individual perspectives in a consensus artifact to foster design focus.

- The territory map serves a critical role in building team dynamic and cohesiveness for collaborative work.

- A speculative vision of the future is combined, including the key people who may be involved in the design landscape to be explored.

- Constructed early in the design process, during planning, scoping, and definition, the map drives ideas for research and design.

- Territory maps may be drafted in a collaborative effort, or each member can consider their contributions first and then bring them to the group.

See also   Stakeholder Maps

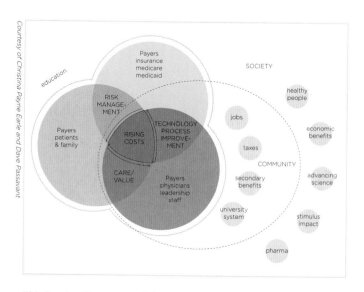

This is a territory map of the landscape of healthcare to determine how design solutions can streamline efficiencies.

086

Thematic Networks

A step-by-step process to identify, organize, and connect common themes in qualitative data

- Systematically breaking down texts into patterns, themes, and relationships helps to synthesize qualitative information into actionable design insight.

- Three classes of themes summarize and organize information into a web-like illustration to communicate findings with stakeholders:

  1. Basic themes come directly from textual data, considered within the context of other basic themes to flesh out a fuller story.

  2. Organizing themes separate basic themes into clusters of similar issues, collectively forming a higher order premise as an argument, position, or assertion.

  3. Global themes distill the overarching point of the text into a single statement, articulating the deeper meaning and complexity of the data.

- Thematic networks help make sense of rich, textual data collected from methods such as diary studies, directed storytelling, or interviews.

See also   Affinity Diagramming • Content Analysis • Exploratory Research

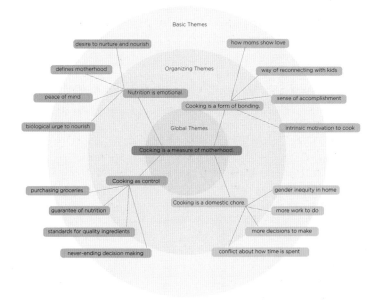

Thematic network analysis provides a methodology that can help researchers work through the challenges of analyzing textual data using a formulaic, step-by-step methodology.

087

Think-Aloud Protocol

Participants verbalize what they are doing and thinking as they complete a task

- This is among the most common evaluative methods in the usability community, revealing aspects of an interface that delight, confuse, or frustrate.

- It asks people to articulate what they are doing, thinking, or feeling as they complete a set of tasks that align with their realistic day-to-day goals.

- Concurrent think-aloud is most common, asking the participant to work through tasks while articulating what he or she is doing, thinking, and feeling.

- Retrospective think-aloud asks participants to complete a task in silence and then comment on their processes as they watch a recorded replay of their experience. This can provide additional insight into participant reasoning, intentions, and strategy.

- The method can be used on low- or high-fidelity prototypes, physical artifacts that require assembly, devices to be synchronized, or customized products.

See also   Desirability Testing • Prototyping • Usability Testing

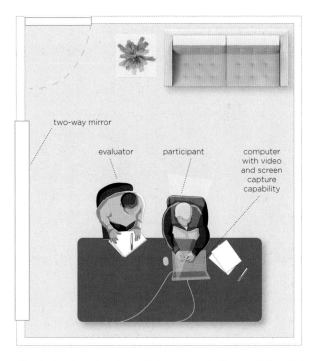

In a think-aloud protocol, participants verbalize anything that they think, feel, do, or look at while processing a prototype or interface to complete tasks.

088

Time-Aware Research

A moderated, remote testing method engaging a real person in real time, just as he or she is about to complete a task

- In contrast to traditional usability testing where tasks are preselected by researchers, time-aware research happens "just in time" to observe a task of interest.

- Live recruiting intercepts participants at the precise moment that they set out to complete a self-directed task, providing insight into how they accomplish goals.

- Using screen-sharing software, this method enables the usability test to occur within the context of an individual's native environment or "technological ecosystem."

- This is a more realistic process than lab testing, as participants can access information on websites, by email, or on their calendar.

- Around 1.5% to 2% of visitors who see the screener will complete it; slightly more than 50% will agree to be contacted; of those, around 65% will be able to participate.

See also Experience Sampling Method • Usability Testing • Remote Moderated Research

In "live recruiting" for time-aware research, end users are intercepted by a prompt to participate in a study immediately as they begin a self-directed task.

089

Touchstone Tours

Using artifacts and the environment as touchstones for insightful conversation

- This guided tour is a contextual, empathic method to understand how people organize information and systems using space and cognitive artifacts.

- The exploratory method allows designers to establish familiarity with a territory in early-phase research.

- The participant is asked to guide the researcher through an environment and objects, specific to themes or subjects being explored by the designer.

- Tours can be guided through homes, workspaces or individual rooms, micro or mobile environments such as backpacks and purses, or digital devices and computer desktops.

- Conversation should be guided yet flexible, allowing fluid departures based on highlights selected by the tour guide and attentive observations by the researcher.

- Thoroughly document tours with video, photos, or sketches and a transcript of the conversation.

See also   Artifact Analysis • Contextual Inquiry • Personal Inventories

A touchstone tour in a prototyping lab highlights specialized tools and processes for a design project investigating master-apprentice relationships.

090

Triading

An interviewing technique whereby participants compare sets of three brands, products, or services

- Triading is a powerful interviewing technique that helps to understand how products and services fit into people's existing personal constructs of the world.

- Triading reveals deep-seated attitudes, perceptions, and feelings toward brands, products, and services.

- Either the researcher or the participant selects six to ten familiar and related brands, products, or services representative of a particular domain.

- The participant picks three of the examples (a triad) for discussion and then explains the ways in which they feel two of the three examples differ from the third.

- This process can be repeated with new triads to elicit multiple constructs about the domain.

- When repeated with many participants, a wealth of data emerges, with varied constructs and ratings identified from person to person.

See also   Interviews • Laddering • Semantic Differential

Triading asks: "How do two of these examples differ from the third?"

091

Triangulation

The convergence of multiple methods on the same research question to corroborate evidence from several different angles

- It ensures accuracy of information by combining sources and mitigating the weaknesses of any single method or source.

- The most common occurrence of triangulation is to combine behavioral observation methods with self-report methods such as questionnaires or interviews.

- Self-reported behaviors or attitudes aligned with social norms or research expectations may be contradicted by actual behaviors observed.

- Triangulation may compare physiological data such as heart rate or pupil dilation with self-reported information or observations of visible behaviors.

- Anecdotal information collected through qualitative means can enrich and humanize the abstraction of quantitative results collected through survey data.

- In usability studies, recordings are triangulated across keystroke/mouse inputs, facial expressions, and actions verbalized in think-aloud protocol.

1. Observation data: Video capture

2. Behavioral data: Recorded TV interactions

3. Self-report data: Interviews

In a Microsoft study of television watching, observations and television interactions were used during interviews to correlate behaviors with TV content and events in the environment.

092

Unobtrusive Measures

Physical evidence, archival records, and nonintrusive observations used for design insight

- This method is used to acquire information without direct participant contact.

- Examples of physical trace *erosion* measures include wear patterns in floors or grass indicating preferred pedestrian traffic.

- Examples of *accretion* measures include litter, graffiti, temporary signage, product modifications, or fingerprints to indicate patterns of use.

- Archives are considered unobtrusive measures because they may be accessed without direct contact with participants.

- Observation can be an unobtrusive measure when those being observed do not know it and the researcher has had no input in the situation structure.

- Digital footprints provide indicators of technology use and qualities of social interaction and communication.

- A limitation may be a lack of details about who has contributed to the data being collected and why.

See also Artifact Analysis • Observation • Secondary Research

Trace *erosion* measures are wear-patterns, such as these preferred pathways or "desire lines." Trace *accretion* measures include additive deposits such as graffiti and litter.

093

Usability Report

Empirical evidence outlining which parts of a user interface should be fixed or improved

- Helps teams decide whether a product is usable enough to release or needs revision and further testing, through the following features:
  - Executive summary, describing the most salient and serious usability problems first, with sections tailored to the concerns of any specific groups
  - Total number of problems, including the frequency, impact, and persistence of usability problems, evidenced by screenshots, or participant quotes
  - A list of the most severe and persistent problems.
  - Positive findings that counterbalance problems with a similar number of observed interactions demonstrating good usability
  - Detailed task and scenario descriptions that are robust and representative enough to effectively get at a range of usability error types

See also   Remote Moderated Research • Think-Aloud Protocol • Usability Report

The proprietary platform of User Insight called "Voice" aggregates research documents, discussion guides, participant information, research calendars, and testing artifacts into a secure online repository.

094

Usability Testing

An evaluative method to observe a user's task-based experience with a digital applications

- Identifies frustrating and confusing parts of an interface so that they can be fixed and retested prior to launch.

- Typically employs Think-Aloud Protocol, detecting problems by observing instances where the user:

  1. Understands the task but can't complete it within a reasonable amount of time

  2. Understands the goal, but has to try different approaches to complete the task

  3. Gives up or resigns from the process

  4. Completes a task, but not the specified task

  5. Expresses surprise or delight

  6. Expresses frustration, confusion, or blames themselves for not being able to complete the task

  7. Asserts that something is wrong or doesn't make sense

  8. Makes a suggestion for the interface or the flow of events

See also   Evaluative Research • Stakeholder Walkthrough • Think-Aloud Protocol

Usability tests with few participants can isolate enough problems to help teams confidently decide whether an interface needs to be revised or is ready for release.

095

User Journey Maps

A visualization of human interactions with a multi-channel product or service

- The journey map tells a visual story about an individual's actions, feelings, perceptions, and mindset as they interact with a product or service.

- It should be an honest representation of an experience, including moments of indecision, confusion, frustration, delight, and closure.

- The journey map allows each moment of an interactive experience to be evaluated and improved by design.

- Multiple maps are usually created alongside personas and scenarios, each heavily informed by direct contact with customers who use the product or service.

- The journey map can shift an organization's focus from an operational, system-centered view to the larger, real-world context in which products and services are used.

- The map should be a living document, with reviews by the design team offering questions, ideas, and suggested improvements.

See also   Customer Experience Audit • Personas • Scenarios

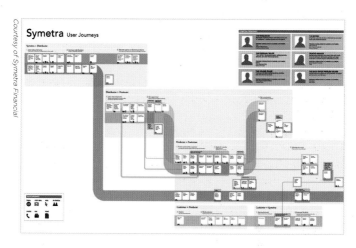

Interviews by digital agency POP resulted in six personas and journeys of Symetra Financial users, ultimately resulting in greater workflow efficiencies through a refreshed website design.

096

Value Opportunity Analysis (VOA)

Mapping the extent to which a product or service's aspirational qualities connect to an audience

- A (VOA) provides an opportunity for a team to work together from a place of deep empathy, grounded firmly in research for what the user values and desires.

- There are seven value opportunities:

  1. Emotion: *adventure, independence, confidence, and power*

  2. Aesthetics: *visual, auditory, tactile, olfactory, and taste*

  3. Identity: *point in time, sense of place, and personality*

  4. Impact: *social and environmental*

  5. Ergonomics: *comfort, safety, and ease of use*

  6. Core Technology: *reliable and enabling*

  7. Quality: *craftsmanship and durability*

- The VOA can be used to help the team consider competitive review, market analysis, and multiple personas.

See also Competitive Testing • Desirability Testing • The Love Letter & the Breakup Letter

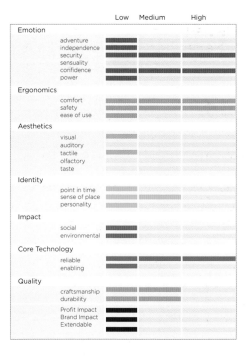

In a VOA, each value opportunity and its attributes are listed in a column and rated on a subjective scale of low, medium, and high.

097

Web Analytics

The collection and analysis of Internet data to understand and optimize web usage

- This process provides a gateway for your organization to become invested in what your customers are doing online and why.

- The first step requires articulating what you want out of the data, expressing your goals and intent for what you want to measure.

- Knowing where you want to go can help you structure your content, analyze campaigns, segment your visitors, and measure your commerce and process tools.

- Translate all of the data into a short report people will want to read, avoiding analytics jargon and visualizing as much data as you can.

- Regularly share reports to internal stakeholders.

- Implement and act on the knowledge, focusing on small course corrections that can have a big impact.

See also A/B Testing • Key Performance Indicators • Site Search Analytics

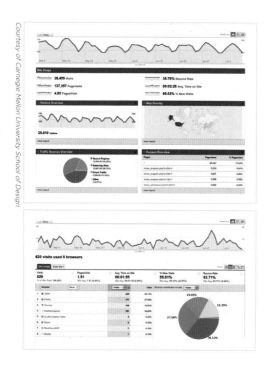

Web analysts will understand your business and the web in equal measure and use tools such as Google Analytics to make recommendations for corrective actions.

098

Weighted Matrix

Identify and prioritize the most promising opportunities from multiple design concepts

- It creates a forum for conversation and shared decision-making and can help overcome the common biases on multidisciplinary teams.

- The underlying concept is simple but powerful: the matrix ranks potential design opportunities against key success criteria.

- The "criteria" represents the primary measures of product success rated on a scale, as defined by the product team and organizational stakeholders.

- A listing of "opportunities" represents the design ideas that elicit the most serious interest from the team.

- Once there is an agreed upon recommended list, another creative "deep dive" can now refocus on newly agreed-upon design ideas.

- The method provides a structured process for team conversations, shifting decision-making to a process grounded in success criteria, not personal opinions.

See also   Design Charette • KJ Technique • Parallel Prototyping

BUSINESS CRITERIA \ IDEAS	WEIGHT	Cargo Organizers	Non-car Accessories	Travel Accessories	Mobilizing Medical Devices	Child Transport
Within Our Companies' Expertise	3	2	3	3	2	2
User Experience	3	2	2	1	3	3
Potential Market Size	2	2	2	3	1	2
Potential for Market Differentiation	2	1	1	2	2	3
Industry Recognition	1	1	1	2	3	3
TOTALS		19	22	24	24	(28)

BUSINESS CRITERIA	WEIGHT	Work Benches	Garage Storage	Rugged Mobility Devices
Within Our Companies' Expertise	3	3	3	2
User Experience	3	2	3	2
Potential Market Size	2	1	3	1
Potential for Market Differentiation	2	1	2	2
Industry Recognition	1	1	2	3
TOTALS		20	(30)	21

A weighted matrix provides a way to manage potential design options by evaluating each design opportunity against business criteria as opposed to personal preferences.

099

Wizard of Oz

Simulated control and response by a researcher behind the scenes, while a participant engages with a system

- Participants are led to believe they are interacting with a working prototype, but in reality, a researcher is acting as a proxy from behind the scenes.

- The "wizard" can intercept and shape the interaction between the participant and the system.

- The goal is to allow a user to realistically experience a product or interface before prototypes are built.

- For an appropriate, timely system response, the researcher must observe participant activity: for example, through video or screen-sharing software.

- The believability of the simulations hinge on the wizard's consistency with respect to timing, patterns, and system logic.

- This is useful when designing applications that do not already have established design patterns (for example, augmented reality or ubiquitous computing).

See also   Experience Prototyping • Speed Dating • Rapid Iterative Testing & Evaluation

Thousands of people have had compelling interactions with the animatronic character Quasi the Robot without knowing that behind the scenes, a human actor controls the robot.

100

Word Clouds

Information visualization that organizes text-based content into interesting arrangements

- Text collages that show the most frequently used words in just about any text-based document.

- Words are assigned different font sizes; usually, the bigger the word, the more frequently it occurs.

- Clouds are made engaging through various dimensions such as typeface, font size, colors, and number of words, word proximity, and word orientation.

- Qualify where word cloud data came from, collection methods, what the fonts, colors, sizes, etc. mean, and disclosure of any data scrubbing or segmenting.

- When archiving transcripts, the visual markers of each cloud create a gestalt unique to each transcript that can facilitate recall.

- Word clouds can be a lighthearted way to engage stakeholders in discussion about the gist of transcripts before delving into more rigorous analysis techniques.

See also   Content Analysis • Exploratory Research • Interviews

Here is a word cloud generated from interviews with parents of picky eaters. When segmented based on meaningful criteria, word clouds can reveal potentially insightful and surprising themes.

References & Notes

05 Automated Remote Research
Bolt, N., and T. Tulathimutte. *Remote Research: Real Users, Real Time, Real Research.* Brooklyn, NY: Rosenfeld Media, 2010.

06 Behavioral Mapping
Sommer, R., and B. Baker Sommer. *A Practical Guide to Behavioral Research: Tools and Techniques.* New York, NY: Oxford University Press, 2002.

07 Bodystorming
Burns, C., et al. "Actors, Hairdos & Videotape—Informance Design: Using Performance Techniques in Multidisciplinary, Observation-based Design." In *CHI 94 Conference Companion*, 1994: 119–120.

08 Brainstorm Graphic Organizers
Hyerle, D. *Visual Tools for Constructing Knowledge.* Alexandria, VA: ASCD, 1996.

11 Case Studies
Robson, C. *Real World Research: A Resource for Social Scientists and Practitioner-Researchers,* 2nd ed. Oxford: Blackwell Publishers, 2002.

12 Cognitive Mapping
Ackermann, F., et al. "Getting Started with Cognitive Mapping" in *The Young OR Conference, University of Warwick,* 1992: 65–82.

13 Cognitive Walkthrough
Wharton, C., et al. "The Cognitive Walkthrough: A Practitioner's Guide" in *Usability Inspection Methods.* New York, NY: John Wiley and Sons, 1994.

19 Contextual Design
Holtzblatt, K., et al. *Rapid Contextual Design: A How-To Guide to Key Techniques for User-Centered Design.* San Francisco, CA: Morgan Kaufmann, 2004.

20 Contextual Inquiry
Holtzblatt, K., and H. Beyer. *Contextual Design: A Customer-Centered Approach to Systems Design.* San Francisco, CA: Morgan Kaufmann, 1998.

23 Crowdsourcing
Kittur, A., et al., Palo Alto Research Center. "Crowdsourcing for Usability: Using Micro-Task Markets for Rapid, Remote, and Low-Cost User Measurements," 2007, www.parc.com/content/attachments/crowdsourcing_user_studies_6280_parc.pdf

24 Cultural Probes
Gaver, B., T. Dunne, and E. Pacenti. "Cultural Probes." *Interactions,* January-February 1999, pp. 21–29.

29 Desirability Testing
Barnum, C. M., and L. A. Palmer. "More Than a Feeling: Understanding the Desirability Factor in User Experience." in *Proceedings of CHI 2010* (2010): 4703–4715.

31 Directed Storytelling
Evenson, S. "Directed Storytelling: Interpreting Experience for Design" in *Design Studies: Theory and Research in Graphic Design, A Reader.* New York, NY: Princeton Architectural Press, 2006: 231–240.

32 Elito Method
Ulrich, E. "Inclusive Iterations: How a Design Team Builds Shared Insights." *UX Week Podcast,* 2007.

33 Ergonomic Analysis
Tannen, R. "Crimping Tools: An Ergonomic Review of the State-of-the-Art." White paper for Thomas & Betts, June 2009.

35 Evidence-based Design
Scupelli, P., et al. "Architecture and Information Technology as Factors in Surgical Suite Information Sharing and Coordination." in *Proceedings of the 1st ACM International Health Informatics Symposium*, 2010: 265–274.

36 Experience Prototyping
Buchenau, M., and J. F. Suri. "Experience Prototyping" in *Proceedings of Designing Interactive Systems (DIS)*. ACM, 2000: 424–433.

38 Experiments
Larson, A. M., and L. C. Loschky. "The Contributions of Central Versus Peripheral Vision to Scene Gist Recognition." *Journal of Vision* 9, no. 10 (2009): 1-16.

42 Fly-on-the-Wall Observation
Zeisel, J. *Inquiry by Design: Environment/Behavior/Neuroscience in Architecture, Interiors, Landscape, and Planning.* New York, NY: Norton, 2006.

46 Heuristic Evaluation
Ginsburg, S. *Designing the iPhone User Experience.* Boston, MA: Addison Wesley, 2010.

Nielsen, J. *Usability Engineering.* Boston, MA: Academic Press, 1993.

49 KJ Technique
Kawakita, J. *The Original KJ Method.* Tokyo: Kawakita Research Institute, 1982.

Spool, J. "The KJ-Technique: A Group Process for Establishing Priorities," 2004, www.uie.com

50 Kano Analysis
Kano, N., et al. "Attractive Quality and Must-be Quality." *Journal of the Japanese Society for Quality Control* 14, no. 2 (1984): 39–48.

Zultner, R. E., and G. H. Mazur. "The Kano Model: Recent Developments." in *The Eighteenth Symposium on Quality Function Deployment*, 2006: 109-116.

51 Key Performance Indicators
Peterson, E. *The Big Book of Key Performance Indicators*, 2006, www.webanalyticsdemystified.com

52 Laddering
Reynolds, T. J., and J. Gutman. "Laddering Theory, Method, Analysis, and Interpretation." *Journal of Advertising Research* 28 (1988): 11–31.

Wansink, B., and N. Chan. "Using Laddering to Understand and Leverage a Brand's Equity." *Qualitative Market Research—An International Journal* 6, no.2 (2003).

54 The Love Letter & The Breakup Letter
https://vimeo.com/11854531

55 Mental Model Diagrams
Young, I. *Mental Models: Aligning Design Strategy with Human Behavior.* Brooklyn, NY: Rosenfeld Media, 2008.

56 Mind Mapping
Hyerle, D. *Visual Tools for Constructing Knowledge.* Alexandria, VA: ASCD, 1996.

58 Parallel Prototyping
Dow, S. P., et al. "Parallel Prototyping Leads to Better Design Results, More Divergence, and Increased Self-Efficacy." *ACM Transactions on Computer-Human Interaction* 17, no. 4 (2010).

59 Participant Observation
Zeisel, J. *Inquiry by Design: Environment/*

Behavior/Neuroscience in Architecture, Interiors, Landscape, and Planning. New York: Norton, 2006.

60 Participatory Action Research (PAR)
McNiff, J. *Action Research for Professional Development*, 2002, www.jeanmcniff.com/ar-booklet.asp

61 Participatory Design
Kuhn, S., and T. Winograd. "Participatory Design" in *Bringing Design to Software*, New York: Addison-Wesley, 1996.

Sanders, E. B.-N., et al. "A Framework for Organizing the Tools and Techniques of Participatory Design" in *Participatory Design Conference (PDC) Proceedings*, 2010: 195-198.

62 Personal Inventories
Blevis, E., and E. Stolterman. "Ensoulment and Sustainable Interaction Design" in *Proceedings of International Association of Design Research Societies Conference IASDR 2007.* Hong Kong: HKPT, 2007.

63 Personas
Cooper, A. *The Inmates Are Running the Asylum: Why High-Tech Products Drive Us Crazy and How to Restore the Sanity.* Indianapolis, IN: Sams–Pearson Education, 2004.

65 Picture Cards
The Picture Cards method was developed by Adaptive Path, www.adaptivepath.com

Kaptelinin, V., and B. A. Nardi. *Acting with Technology: Activity Theory and Interaction Design.* Cambridge, MA: The MIT Press, 2006.

68 Rapid Iterative Testing & Evaluation
Medlock, M. C., et al. "Using the RITE Method to Improve Products: A Definition and a Case Study" in *UPA Conference Proceedings*, 2002.

69 Remote Moderated Research
Bolt, N., and T. Tulathimutte. *Remote Research: Real Users, Real Time, Real Research.* San Francisco, CA: Rosenfeld Media, 2010.

70 Research Through Design
Burdick, A. "Design (as) Research" in *Design Research: Methods and Perspectives*, Cambridge, MA: MIT Press, 2003: 82.

Zimmerman, J., et al. "Research Through Design as a Method for Interaction Design Research in HCI." In *Proceedings of CHI*, ACM, 2007: 493-502.

72 Scenario Description Swimlanes
Yvonne Shek at nForm adapted swimlanes as an activity diagram of the Unified Modeling Language (UML) in 2007.

75 Semantic Differential
Osgood, C., et al. *The Measurement of Meaning.* Urbana, IL: University of Illinois Press, 1957.

78 Site Search Analytics
Rosenfeld, L. *Search Analytics for Your Site: Conversations With Your Customers.* Brooklyn, NY: Rosenfeld Media, 2011.

79 Speed Dating
Davidoff, S., et al. "Rapidly Exploring Application Design Through Speed Dating." in *Proceedings of 9th International Conference on Ubiquitous Computing UbiComp '07*, 2007: 429-446.

81 Stakeholder Walkthrough
Karat, C.-M., et al. "Comparison of Empirical Testing and Walkthrough Methods in User Interface Evaluation." in *Proceedings of the SIGCHI Conference on Human Factors in Computing Systems*, 1992: 397-404.

82 Storyboards
Truong, K. N., et al. "Storyboarding: An Empirical Determination of Best Practices and Effective Guidelines." in *Proceedings of DIS 2006*, 2006: 12-21

84 Task Analysis
Kirwan, B., and L. K. Ainsworth. *A Guide to Task Analysis*. London; Washington D.C.: Taylor and Francis, 1992: 397-404

Kuniavsky, M. *Observing the User Experience: A Practitioner's Guide to User Research*. San Franciscon, CA: Morgan Kaufmann, 2003.

86 Thematic Networks
Attride-Stirling, J. "Thematic Networks: An Analytic Tool for Qualitative Research." *Qualitative Research* 1, no. 3 (2001): 385–405.

87 Think-aloud Protocol
Guan, Z., et al. "The Validity of Stimulated Retrospective Think-Aloud Method as Measured by Eye Tracking." in *CHI 2006 Conference Proceedings*, 2006: 1253-1262.

88 Time-aware Research
Bolt, N., and T. Tulathimutte. *Remote Research: Real Users, Real Time, Real Research*. Brooklyn, NY: Rosenfeld Media, 2010.

92 Unobtrusive Measures
Webb, E. J., et al. *Unobtrusive Measures: Nonreactive Research in the Social Sciences*. Chicago: Rand McNally, 1966. Revised edition, Thousand Oaks, CA: Sage Publications, 2000.

94 Usability Testing
Jacobsen, N. E., et al. "The Evaluator Effect in Usability Studies: Problem Detection and Severity Judgments." in *Proceedings of the Human Factors and Ergonomics Society 42nd Annual Meeting*, 1998: 1336-1340

96 Value Opportunity Analysis
Cagan, J., and C. Vogel. *Creating Breakthrough Products: Innovation from Product Planning to Program Approval*. Upper Saddle River, NJ: Prentice Hall, 2002.

97 Web Analytics
Peterson, E. *Web Analytics Demystified*, 2004, www.webanalyticsdemystified.com

Burby, J. *Three Reasons Analytics Fail Companies*, 2004, www.clickz.com

98 Weighted Matrix
Cagan, J., and C. Vogel. *Creating Breakthrough Products: Innovation from Product Planning to Program Approval*. Upper Saddle River, NJ: Prentice Hall, 2002.

99 Wizard of Oz
Kelly, J. F. "An Iterative Design Methodology for User-Friendly Natural Language Office Information Applications." *ACM Transactions on Office Information Systems* 2, no. 1 (1984): 26–41.

Brimming with creative inspiration, how-to projects, and useful information to enrich your everyday life, Quarto Knows is a favorite destination for those pursuing their interests and passions. Visit our site and dig deeper with our books into your area of interest: Quarto Creates, Quarto Cooks, Quarto Homes, Quarto Lives, Quarto Drives, Quarto Explores, Quarto Gifts, or Quarto Kids.

© 2018 Quarto Publishing Group USA Inc.

Text © 2018 Bruce Harrington and Bella Martin

First Published in 2018 by Rockport Publishers, an imprint of The Quarto Group,

100 Cummings Center, Suite 265-D, Beverly, MA 01915, USA.

T (978) 282-9590 F (978) 283-2742 QuartoKnows.com

Rockport Publishers titles are also available at discount for retail, wholesale, promotional, and bulk purchase. For details, contact the Special Sales Manager by email at specialsales@quarto.com or by mail at The Quarto Group, Attn: Special Sales Manager, 100 Cummings Center, Suite 265-D, Beverly, MA 01915, USA.

10 9 8 7 6 5 4 3

ISBN: 978-1-63159-374-1

Cover: Coa Design

Page Layout: Tabula Rasa Graphic Design

Getty Images: Method 90

Shutterstock.com: Methods 4, 11, 39, 42, 48, 54, 62, and 94

Printed in China

MIX
Paper from
responsible sources
FSC® C101537